THE BAMBOO GR

AN INTRODUCTION TO SIJO

山前에 有臺ᄒᆞ고 臺下애 有水ᅵ로

다뻬만 흐를매 기노오 녕가 녕ᄒᆞ여

든엇다 나ᄒᆞᆞ 白駒ᄂᆞᆫ 머리 모솜ᄒᆞ

ᄂᆞ고

其六

春風에 花滿山ᄒᆞ고 秋夜애 月滿臺

라 四時佳興ᅵ 사름과 ᄒᆞᆫ가지라ᄒᆞ

ᄂᆞᆯ 뎌 魚躍鳶飛雲影天光이 샤어ᄂᆞᅵ

그지 이슬고

THE BAMBOO GROVE

AN INTRODUCTION TO SIJO

edited and translated by
RICHARD RUTT

Ann Arbor
THE UNIVERSITY OF MICHIGAN PRESS

2001   2000   1999   1998   4   3   2   1

ISBN 0-472-08558-1

Earlier versions of seventy-eight of these translations were previously
published in Volume XXXIV of the *Transactions of the Royal Asiatic
Society, Korea Branch*, 1958. Thirty-eight of the poems also appeared in
earlier versions in *Asia*, No. 9, Fall, 1967, and twelve of them in *Yesul
chŏnghwa* ("Korea Through Her Arts"), published in Seoul in 1964. Some
others have appeared occasionally in the *Korea Times*. One section of the
Introduction is based on part of an article on the nature of classical sijo,
published in *Korea Journal*, Vol. IV, No. 4 (April, 1964).

to
DAVID

The wind is pure and clear,
                the moon is pure and bright.
The bamboo grove within the pines
                is pure of worldly cares:
But a lute and piles of scrolls
                can make it purer still.

KWŎN HOMUN (1532–1587)

I am grateful to the living poets and representatives of poets who gave permission for the translation and publication of modern sijo. I regret that it was impossible to get in touch with appropriate persons in two or three cases, although every effort was made.

The Korean printing on the title page is part of the woodblocks mentioned at the bottom of page 157. It gives the texts of sijos 175 and 176 in this volume.

R. R.

FOREWORD: THE BAMBOO GROVE, HABITAT OF MOST COLORFUL BIRDS

David R. McCann

Published nearly thirty years ago, Richard Rutt's collection of *sijo* songs made and makes a richly rewarding experience of literature and literary culture. It is a marvelous collection of poems, translated with a quite palpable sense of appreciation for their cultural contexts, of where the songs came from, how they utilized the nuances of Korean language while manipulating the array of Chinese literary and historical references that have comprised such significant markings in Korean cultural history, and of how they still occupy a lively space in contemporary Korea.

The translations state their own cumulative case as literary works, and I leave that aspect of their appreciation to the reader's encounter with the collection. As I put the matter rather woodenly some time ago, "The book is a real pleasure to read, in large part because of the combination of alert enthusiasm and extensive familiarity with the subject that Rutt brings to this study of *sijo* verse" (*Harvard Journal of Asiatic Studies* 33 [1973]: 272). On this happy occasion, the republication of the book, I shall venture instead to two general topics that Rutt's notes on form, style, history, and other matters have led me. I hope my brief explorations of these subjects may provoke thought, discussion, and continued, or repeated, reading of this and other gatherings of Korean poetry.

Korean History

The view of Korean history that might be derived from a reading of these *sijo* songs, especially those in the first section, "Historical Songs," is of a narrative characterized by sudden, violent changes, upheavals that have summoned up, in turn, the expressions of determined loyalty that characterize many of the first group of songs. Two events in particular seem to have provided the stimuli for these songs: the ending of the Koryŏ dynasty (918–1392) and beginning of Chosŏn (1392–1910), and the usurpation of the Korean throne by Sejo (r. 1455–1468), who engineered the exile and death of his own nephew, the boy king Tanjong (1441–1457; r. 1452–1455). The end of Koryŏ was a particularly nasty affair, with sons of monks acceding to the throne and disenfranchised members of the Wang royal house being reinstated only long enough to be royally purged, in a sequence of events that left most of the ruling groups caught in a swirling tide of conflicted loyalties. Compounding the problems was the unsettled nature of Koryŏ's relationship to the rulers of what we now call China. As the Sung dynasty struggled against and then succumbed to Ming, where did Korean loyalties lie? Songs number 1 and 56 (the famous *sijo* song by Chŏng Mongju) engage the issue of loyalty and change, and seem, as it were, to have set off a scattershot burst of similar expressions of loyalty some sixty years later, when Korean domestic affairs of state were once again riven by a struggle over the succession.

What can we infer from this pattern? Loyalty in traditional Korean culture, as in most others, was highly prized. That it was so vociferously and often asserted might suggest that political exigencies had already placed it in rather short supply. Factional struggles in the later centuries of the Chosŏn dynasty replaced the succession struggles, but were no less lethal to those caught up in them. The eighteenth-century King Yŏngjo struggled to reimpose some sense of order on the domestic government, hoping (against hope) that personal rectitude and a strong, renewed emphasis on the virtues of filiality might bring things around. Vain hope! The king was constrained to have his own son executed for his dangerously criminal behavior. No wonder, then, that the shadow theme of rustication, of withdrawal from the contentious official world and pursuit of the life of quiet, rural contemplation, became such a favorite in Korean *sijo*. The "Drinking Songs" (numbers 21–30), "Songs of Music" (102–104), "Songs of Nature"

(118–148), and "Songs of Retirement and Rustic Life" (149–222) all bespeak the attractiveness of the life away from court and public office, away from history.

Or do they? Rutt's account of the literary innovations in Yun Sŏndo's (1587–1671) "The Fisherman's Calendar" (183–222) makes clear its significance as a literary work, as does his assignment of the usual political reading of the work to a simple footnote (210: . . . "The reference is political: Yun is retired from government life and service.") It is true enough that everything in Korean life was political, at least for the ruling class, but do the *sijo* songs in this collection and elsewhere reflect nothing but politics and the individual's reaction to it? By steadily directing the reader's attention to the literary rather than political elements of the works, Rutt argues implicitly for the predominance of the aesthetic criterion and for recognition of the constructed nature of historical narrative in which the works are situated.

There are numerous hints, structural as well as explicitly expository, that the history in this collection is of a piece with the works seen or heard as (oral) literature. One striking instance is the *sijo* song ascribed to the *kisaeng*, or female entertainer, Hwang Chini (sixteenth century), "This is all my doing! / Did I not know I loved him so?" (70) The song is situated in the "Love Songs" section of the book, where it finds itself in company with a number of others, most of them anonymous or ascribed to Hwang Chini and other *kisaeng*. Yet the note to number 70 observes "Some editions attribute this poem to King Sŏngjong (reigned 1470–1494). In that case it is understood to express regret over the dismissal of a minister." Notice how easily the substitution is made: king for *kisaeng*, highest occupant of the social scale for the lowest, male for female, fifteenth century for sixteenth. *History* proves to be a most malleable substance indeed, in the realm of the *sijo*.

That the songs and their associated stories survived through oral performance rather than in a formal, written record until the eighteenth century, at which point they began to be gathered into a series of music anthologies, begins to suggest the outlines of another realm of history entirely: not the official historical records written in Chinese but the subversive, vernacular Korean record. Statements in this realm were powerful and personal rather than careful and public. It became the realm of all the people and seems to have been the realm of the heart, not head, where even the most carefully composed public figures were said to have uttered, whispered, shouted or sung what the songs record. Glimpsing this realm behind, as it were, the quasi-historical narrative fragments that traditionally accompany the *sijo* songs prompts a series of questions. To what extent were the public figures represented in the *sijo* tradition in some literal sense *composed?* Might historical figures and names have been connected ex post facto to the *sijo* they were said, but never recorded, to have uttered? Is it not possible, as a recent essay suggests, that the "author" of Chŏng Mongju's intensely famous song of loyalty was a woman vowing loyalty to her Koryŏ royal lover, just as Hwang Chini's song (70) is also ascribed to a king?

It makes a great deal of sense to look at the many examples of songs of retirement as comprising a literary genre rather than a political move. One might then ask if there is not some affinity between the *sijo* form and certain subjects, or tones of voice, such as one might observe in the case of a verse form like the limerick. Or returning for the moment to the beginning of these ruminations on history, might the *determined loyalty* expressed in many *sijo* songs be *determined* in another sense: by the narrative constraints of the traditional story in which the song is imbedded? It is the story of Chŏng Mongju's loyalty to Koryŏ that requires his refusal of the Yi family's blandishments.

Sijo and Translation

The large gap between event and record, in the case of the *sijo* songs and their associated stories, along with the oral realm of their provenance, locates the *sijo* as a genre—whether historical songs, songs of music, of solitude, or any of the other categories of the collection—in the same area of Korean literature as the oral-narrative *p'ansori*. This provenance is not, however, ahistorical or antihistorical, despite the general tendency in literary studies to denigrate or dismiss that which is oral.

The 1970s and 1980s saw a major development in Korean historiography, the articulation and pursuit of a study that attended to the life conditions and narratives of the common people, or marginalized groups, the *minjung*, as opposed to the histories of the elites that had previously commanded the attention of the scholarly community. This recent shift moved over the same ground as that which lies between such literary forms as the vernacular *sijo* or *p'ansori* and the vast accumulation of works written prior to the twentieth century in Classical Chinese. The *minjung* movement also rearticulates the contrast between the twelfth-century *History of the Three Kingdoms, Samguk sagi*, with its concern for matters of official state record, cast in the form of the Chinese histories, and the thirteenth-century compilation or miscellany of stories, songs, poems, myth, genealogies, and other materials known as *Remnants of the Three Kingdoms, Samguk yusa*. The word *yusa, remnants*, can be read quite pointedly as a reference to the *sagi*, in the sense that what remained after the official history had been compiled were the heterogenous materials that comprise the *yusa*.

To return to the *sijo:* they remind us not only that Korean history was full as any with strife, murderous betrayals, and brave statements of loyalty, but that the history is itself a highly contested realm of discourse, with the dominant side at any given moment seeking to impose its view of events on the official record, while the other found expression in such forms as the *sijo*. This can appear directly as a matter of the contested historical record. It can also appear less directly in other topics or subject areas, such as the love songs in the present collection, or the deliciously deconstructive *sasŏl sijo* that occupy the next-to-last section in the book. These songs remind us that the vernacular was already subversive in a cultural and political system that made such extensive use of the Chinese model. The subversive potential of the vernacular was recognized and clearly understood

from the moment when King Sejong promulgated the Korean al-
phabet, as a group of officials led by Ch'oe Malli vigorously ob-
jected to a medium that would permit mere clerks and other low
types to circumvent the training in Chinese letters that com-
prised the curriculum for state service appointment. But how de-
licious, I cannot resist saying, was the result! Where pompous
thoughts indeed could be pressed into a *sijo* song, as witness the
mercifully brief selection of "Moral Songs," a *sasŏl sijo* such as
number 232, "Of all the birds and all the beasts / the cock and the
dog are the ones to get rid of" quite literally bursts apart the for-
mal conventions of voice, tone, and attitude. Do Confucian famil-
ial practices seem inevitably to require an overbearing mother-
in-law? Given that formal context, the song "How did it happen?
However did it happen? / Oh mother-in-law, what shall I do?"
(235) is a hilarious send-up. As the note observes, "A considerate
mother-in-law was a contradiction of all traditional probability.
The poem is therefore satirical."

From the subversively satirical to the problematically loyalist,
the *sijo* genre has incorporated features and attributes that seem
almost to cry out to the more theoretically minded to take a look.
Lawrence Venuti, in *The Translator's Invisibility: A History of
Translation* (Routledge, 1995, 307) arguing against the goal of
transparency in translation, the attempt to convey, in translation,
what is merely identical in the other language and culture, writes
as follows:

> (M. Blanchot) . . . considers the foreign text, not as the un-
> changing cultural monument in relation to which the transla-
> tion must forever be an inadequate, ephemeral copy, but as a
> text in transit, "never stationary," . . . constituting a powerful
> self-difference which translation can release or capture in a
> unique way.

Translated to the present book, Blanchot and Venuti might be
heard to assert that the *sijo* presents a text that moves through
performance, through an oral history of transition, and interro-

gates, in its passage, the cultural and political-historical frames in which it appears. By remaining alert to that dynamic, and by alerting the reader to it, Rutt manages to capture and release—banded, to be sure, in English—a remarkably colorful bird indeed.

PREFACE TO THE ANN ARBOR
PAPERBACKS EDITION

It is over forty years since these translations were begun by candlelight in a postwar winter at Anjung, a market village near P'yŏngt'aek. Two years earlier, in 1954, I had arrived in Korea fresh from Cambridge, my head full of sonnets by Petrarch and Camões, eager to encounter Korean poetry. No guidance was available from foreign friends, and I could neither read nor speak Korean. To make some sort of beginning, while I was exploring the potholed streets of Seoul, I scanned the contents of its countless little bookshops for anything with the Chinese character *si* ("poetry") in its title. When I found myself alone in Anjung, I picked from these gleanings the poetry book that seemed best suited to my ignorance: a pretty paperback called *Kogŭm myŏngsijo chŏnghae* ("Explanation of Famous *Sijo*, Ancient and Modern"), printed in 1954. The blurb said it was designed for students facing college entrance examinations.

The poems were printed using eighteenth-century spelling. Though the printing was fuzzy and the paper little better than newsprint, the notes were lavish and helpful. The name of the chief compiler, "I Hou," was clearly a pseudonym, apparently meaning "You great fool," but this book turned out to be a lucky choice. "I Hou," a conventionally modest pun, was the pen name of "Yi Hou" (1912–1970), a notable *sijo* poet (No. 247 in *The Bamboo Grove* was written by him) and his texts were taken from *Kosijo chŏnghae* ("Explanation of Old *Sijo*") published in 1949 by the pioneer scholar Pang Chonghyŏn (1905–1952).

When a lecture I had given to the Royal Asiatic Society in December 1957 was printed in the Society's *Transactions* the following summer, I listed the other books I used. They were nearly all schoolbooks. Comprehensive scholarly books critically unraveling the variant texts of old *sijo* did not appear for another decade.

As I became familiar with the subject, I realized that some of the short poems translated by James Scarth Gale and Homer

Bezaleel Hulbert in the 1890s were originally *sijo*. They were scarcely recognizable, because both men had turned them into romantic Victorian epigrams, and both regarded the songs as inferior because they were not written in Chinese. Later on I was to value Gale's translations of *hanmun*, which were much better than this early work on *sijo*, but at this stage I was more aware of his shortcomings.

Then I came upon the work of Pyŏn Yŏngt'ae (1892–1969). He had been a professor of English for most of his life and was a politician during the early years of the Republic, serving as Prime Minister from 1954 to 1956. His *Songs from Korea* (1948) contained a number of *sijo* in rhymed versions that were no small achievement. They can give much pleasure, but Pyŏn modeled his style on Emily Dickinson. His translations do not convey the spontaneity and vigor of the old songs. I found them de-Koreanized. Even when they deal with rural matters, his interpretations lack the smell of the soil.

The work of Peter Lee, then just beginning his long and distinguished career at the University of Hawaii, was another matter. He had first published some of his fastidious *sijo* translations in the *Hudson Review*, but I saw them after they had been reprinted in *East and West* (Rome 1956). They are still the versions that give me greatest pleasure. If asked to compare them with my own approach, I would say I think there is more mud on my shoes.

My life lay outside academe. Rejoicing in the living tradition of *sijo* around me and always absorbed primarily by my pastoral work, I went on translating for sheer pleasure, without recording the texts with which I had worked. When Bonnie Crown of the Asia Society Literature Programme was visiting Korea and suggested what became *The Bamboo Grove*, I used Chŏ Pyŏnguk's *Sijo munhak sajon* ("Dictionary of *Sijo* Literature," 1966) to check some details (by no means exhaustively) and provide an index to the Korean originals, but I did no more than imply in my note on "texts and sources" that I had not checked my versions with his texts.

Soon after *The Bamboo Grove* appeared, I began to regret that I had not taken the subject more seriously. The most helpful review of the book was by Peter Lee, in the *Journal of Asian Studies* (1972), where he drew attention to a number of errors, most of which could easily have been avoided. Peter stated the facts without rancor—in later years he included some of my work in books he compiled—but even Yi Hou's little book would have helped with some of them. I am glad to apologize now for them and a few others. Very likely there are more, as yet unsignaled.

Among the old short poems lies the phrase "Was it round?" in No. 93. This is an inexplicable way of translating the original "Was it square?" Then in No. 103 "moving the goosefoot" does not make the Great String "sound" but changes the mode. And in the last line of No. 221, where the note and the classical allusion ought to have alerted me, what I took to mean freezing hands really means "counting the days on our fingers."

Errors lie thicker in the *sasŏl sijo*—I remember tackling them with more abandon then when doing the metrically stricter pieces. I left out "in my arms" after "asleep" in No. 232, line 3; and there are several other minor omissions that would be tedious if listed, but betray the same lack of care. Then I was overromantic when I wrote "gentleness" for "coyness" in 223.11, while in 235.3 the girl was not "putting rice into a cauldron" but "getting the boy-friend's rice ready." (Was he the mother-in-law's boyfriend?) In 236.12 I made heavy weather of "pure gold chopsticks engraved with heavenly peaches and hung with blue enameled bells" for "a pure gold ring with pendant blue bell shaped like a heavenly peach," while 242 is really about a white-haired nymphomaniac who wants to seduce a young gentleman, and the poem needs "she" for "he" and "her" for "his."

Among the modern poems, No. 246 needs rewriting. I had misgivings at the time. Ch'oe Namsŏn's work has never set me on fire, but he had to be represented, and the image of the broken inkstone was appealing. The translation was not well done; translators are best advised to work on what moves them. This inkstone could be an image of Korea under Japanese colonial government, and a better translation might be:

When everything falls to pieces
    could this alone stay whole?
It is cracked, no doubt of that,
    yet the inkstone is still an inkstone.
Though well-worn, it is sound at heart—
    would a connoisseur not know that?

Of the correction and amplification of notes there could be no end. No. 157 is a translation of a quatrain by the great Chinese poet Tu Mu, the offering of parsley as sign of humble appreciation in No. 58 is derived from a story in Lieh-tzu, but the value of notes to the reader is probably disproportionately less than the pleasure the compiler gets from unearthing the nuggets they contain. Nevertheless, I ought to have given a reference for the text of the poem on the dedication page. Kwŏn Homun's *sijo* about the bamboo grove is No. 834 in Chŏng Pyŏnguk's *Sijo munhak sajŏn.*

Though I have been back in England and Cornwall for twenty-four years, the first flush of joy on meeting the perfect fusion of word and image in *sijo* has never faded. The discussion of *sijo* craftsmanship in the introduction to *The Bamboo Grove* may make turgid reading, but it shows that there is such craftsmanship, and that it is highly developed. Now I would want to emphasize more strongly the connection between words and music that I underlined in 1971. I am more than ever struck by the redundancy of the last few syllables of each poem—the words that are never sung. How did they get there? Could it have been because copyists wanted the satisfaction of a grammatical sentence ending?

For the same reason, I do not accept the point made by a Korean reviewer who thought I had misunderstood the structure of *sijo* because I printed each poem in three lines rather than six. The Korean convention of printing a *sijo* in three lines was not invented until the twentieth century. Before that, each poem was printed like a prose paragraph, unpunctuated. Though division into three parts is reasonable, and typographically feasible in Korean, it is not so easily manageable in English. Furthermore, tripartite division obscures more fundamental elements in Korean prosody. William Skillend pointed out that each of the three so-called lines is really "a couplet, which is basic to almost all Korean poetry before the twentieth century: two lines, each of two phrases, and each phrase usually of three or four syllables." Six-part division of a *sijo* shows this better and has been preferred by several translators. Bearing in mind my question about the sixth part, if I were now to contemplate rearranging the translations, it would be in the direction of making five lines, not three.

The old poems are now easier to study. Painstaking indexes and comparative texts can be found in Sim Chaewan *Kyobon yŏktae Sijo Chŏnjip* ("Complete Collection of Comparative Historic *Sijo* Texts," 1972), which contains 3,335 poems. Pak Ŭlsu's two compendious volumes of *Han'guk sijo taesajŏn* ("Great Dictionary of Korean *Sijo*," 1991) provide rich bibliographical information and 5,492 poems. What English-language readers need next, perhaps, are studies of the various historic anthologies and of the relationship between *sijo* and Korean experience of lyric poetry in Chinese. The field has barely been opened.

I am not aware that anyone has seriously studied the oral tradition in *sijo*. It may still not be too late to take up the subject. There must have been thousands of *sijo* that were never recorded. The text of No. 90 may or may not be very old—at least the opening phrase is a traditional one. So far as I know, it has not been printed. I took it down from an old gentleman on the Pusan-Seoul express about 1967.

Uyŏnhi chinadaga
    kkot-hyanggi ttara tŭllyŏttŏni
pakkotto tchojiryŏgo
    onŭn nabi kwalsihani
Tongjaya: sin tollyŏ noara
    apkirŭl chaech'okhaji

It is hard to imagine a woman singing with this kind of cynicism. Some of the imagery is conventional (especially the butterflies), but this particular acerbity is not.

Another possibility in the oral tradition is suggested by Hulbert's "bald" translation in *The Passing of Korea* (1906).

> This month, third month, willow becomes green;
> Oriole preens herself;
> Butterfly flutters about.
> Boy, bring zither. Must sing.

The Korean text appears in no anthologies but was printed by Hulbert in *The Korean Repository* (February 1896).

> I tari samwŏrinji
> pŏdŭl pit p'ŭrŭrotta
> kwoekkori kit tadŭmko
> hojyŏp p'ŏlp'ŏl syŏtkyŏnanda
> Ăhăiya komun'go-ryul kollora
> ch'yunhŭnggyŏwi

This is in many ways a conventional spring song.

> This month is the third moon,
> The willows have turned bright green,
> Orioles are preening their plumage,
> butterflies flutter their wings.
> Come here, boy! Get the Black Lute tuned;
> spring has come . . .

But two things redeem what might have been the merest pastiche. Most orioles in *sijo* only sing, while these preen themselves, and asking the boy to tune the lute is more than the usual menial request simply to bring it.

The cult of the unsung *sijo*, the *sijo* never intended to be sung, provides a lively strain in modern writing. It already has a history of some eighty years that will soon be worth study in its own right. When I wrote the introduction to *The Bamboo Grove* a quarter of a century ago, I thought the word *sijo* meaning the words and not the song was first used in the title of Ch'oe Namsŏn's anthology *Sijo yuch'wi* of 1929. I have since discovered that he had used the word that way in 1913, the year of his twenty-third birthday, when, under the name of his brother Ch'angsŏn, he wrote the introduction to *Kagok-sŏn*, a collection of nearly six hundred *sijo* texts edited by Ch'ie Namsŏn under the pseudonym Namakchiun. He is indeed a towering figure in the story of Korea's awakening to the expression of her nationhood in literature.

I am flattered and grateful that Professor McCann has written a foreword to this reprint. The resurrection of the book has naturally opened the floodgates of memory: pleasant conversations with patient Koreans, especially with two distinguished teachers, Cho Yunje and P'i Ch'ŏndŭk, and with the professional *sijo* singer, Hong Wŏn'gi; the delightful visits to Korea of Bonnie Crown, the book's fairy godmother; the life, the landscape, and the atmosphere that the old *sijo* celebrate and that I enjoyed for twenty years; but not least of David, the younger brother I can no longer talk with but with whom I shared the kind of friendship Chinese and Korean poets write about. He was a typographic designer who loved the beauty of books. He died in 1992. If rededication of a book is acceptable, then this second edition must be offered in his memory.

> R. R.
> Falmouth, Cornwall
> Eastertide 1998

CONTENTS

INTRODUCTION

Every morning during the summer months I could look out of my window in Seoul across the crowded tiles of the neighborhood houses, and see the dusty little garden behind the University. Two old men came there soon after dawn. They sat cross-legged on the gnarled roots of an ancient tree and sang *sijo* until it was time to go home for breakfast, slapping their knees with slow rhythmic blows to mark the meter, which ought to have been sounded on a drum. Sometimes their song would be of old age:

> Spring breezes melt the mountain snows,
>> pass by quickly, and then are gone.
> How I wish they would hover,
>> briefly, gently, over my head.
> Melt away the frost of creeping age
>> that greys the hair on my neck.

But younger people sing sijo too. On a sun-drenched summer afternoon I have visited an old mansion, dignified in its decay, near the center of the still rustic city of Suwon, and found there in a cool arbor some leisured folk with well-tended musical instruments. The men, plying bamboo fans to cool themselves, in spite of their translucent grasscloth clothing, stop every now and then between their games of chess and their perusals of the daily newspapers to slide a drum across the floor and suggest to one of the women that she sing a sijo. The languid notes float out across the empty courtyard, as much a part of the old town atmosphere as the sound of a village boy's pipe is part of an autumn evening in Korea's hills. She will probably be singing of love:

> I thought about that fan
>> and why you sent it to me . . .
> You must have meant me
>> to puff out the flame in my heart.
> But my tears cannot quench it,
>> so what use will a fan be?

1

These are amateurs with time to spare for mastering the art of singing sijo. They would be delighted to sing such poems, possibly even to compose them for the occasion, at a wedding banquet or a party held to honor a distinguished guest. They continue a tradition which has remained alive in Korea since the fifteenth century. There are also professional performers in the same tradition today. They cut long-playing discs of sijo, they perform on the radio, they sing for the soundtracks of historical films—classical sijo have even been used as the themes for whole films and novels.

But the sijo tradition has another aspect in modern Korea. In the country markets you can buy long printed strips of cheap facsimile calligraphy, which are the poorer people's substitute for scrolls of writing. They are often used to eke out the wallpaper in a farmer's house or in the guestrooms of a buddhist temple, and very frequently the wording is a sijo. Here the didactic poems and the songs of moral inspiration come into their own, though the world-weary and cynical songs are by no means unwelcome, even among the least sophisticated. Every schoolboy can recite some of them. While you are having your shoes polished by some scruffy little lad in a faded school uniform and a broken cap, just murmur the first words of Chŏng Mongju's:

> Though this frame should die and die . . .

Without fail you will get a delighted grin as the boy takes up:

> though I die a hundred times . . .

and recites it through to the end.

Classical singing has become a highbrow pleasure, but the poetry itself is everybody's property. In earlier days sijo were sung and enjoyed only in the court and great houses of the aristocracy. Few were printed except as texts and anthologies for the singers, who, then as now, were either gentlemen enjoying a gentlemanly hobby or professionals who had learned court music from an early age. Often the subject of their songs was the rustic life; usually the tone was nostalgic, longing for an escape into a rustic peace that scarcely existed. Even in the late nineteenth century the king and queen of Korea would sometimes retire to their version of the Petit Trianon, a huge old farmhouse built in a corner of the Secret Gardens of the Summer Palace in Seoul. There they would relax with simple meals of grain, herbs, and seaweed cooked by the queen's own hands. Their aspirations are often heard in sijo:

> You need not spread that straw mat:
> > can I not sit on fallen leaves?
> Nor light that pinewood torch:
> > the moon is up that sank last night.
> Don't argue, boy, the wine may be sour,
> > and served with weeds, but pour it.

However, the real folksongs of the people at the same period were telling a different story. It was a story of the grim insecurity of the farmer's life. To a gay melody the peasant singer improvised ironical ditties of sickness and extortion, of domestic tragedy and false lovers, as well as of the touching beauty of the scenery and the simple delights of watching village maidens searching for roots on the mountainside in spring, or young people playing rustic games in the autumn. The melodies were strong and the rhythms simple. Their style underlies the pop songs and the military marches that are blared forth on loudspeakers in Korean city streets today. The sinuous melodies of the sijo belonged to a more aristocratic tradition, and hold a different place in Korea's evolving culture.

The sijo, like the folksong, is often anonymous, but it is a more delicate work. There is fine poetic craftsmanship in the best sijo, and this is why the form, like other forms of lyric poetry, both oriental and western, has been able to live as well without its music as with it. The shoeshine boys, like thousands of other Koreans, learn the lyrics without their difficult tunes, and enjoy them none the less for that.

Before the eighteenth century the composition of poetry was not limited to professional poets. Korea, like other Far Eastern countries, trained all educated men in literature and composition. Poetry, whether in Korean or Chinese, was written by all men

3

engaged in public life, even in military service. The resulting corpus of poetry is very different from the poetry of the West. Because the composers were not professional poets, their work tended to be less adventurous and more formalized than the work of western poets. There was little experimentation with forms, which showed less development than one would expect during a comparable period of time in the history of western poetry. Several traditional Chinese stanza patterns were used in Korea, but from the fifteenth century onwards poems written in the Korean language had only two possible forms. One was the *kasa*, composed of an indefinite number of verses, not usually arranged in stanzas, in which each verse consisted of two four-syllable phrases. The other was the sijo.

The earliest sijo extant are attributed to the late Koryŏ dynasty —the end of the fourteenth century. There is no generally accepted theory about why the sijo should suddenly have appeared at that time, although some elements in the form can be discovered in earlier and cruder vernacular verse forms. The sijo traditionally dated as of the Koryŏ period are conventional in their imagery and most of them have political references. Their authors were men of the Koryŏ capital, Kaesŏng, in central Korea. Ever since that time very few sijo have been written by persons who live further north, apart from a handful by *kisaeng*, the professional entertaining women. This was partly a result of the political policy of the Yi dynasty, which inhibited the development of culture in the north and encouraged the development of music and the performing arts most particularly in the southernmost areas, where styles of sijo singing distinctive of the Kyŏngsang and Chŏlla provinces developed alongside the Seoul style.

Halfway through the fifteenth century the Korean alphabet was invented, and from then on Korean-language compositions could be accurately recorded. If the traditional attributions are correct, some of the most attractive of all sijo were written between the time of the invention of the alphabet and the time of the Japanese invasions at the end of the sixteenth century. Political themes were still common, but the imagery was more imaginative, espe-

4

cially in the works of Chŏng Ch'ŏl. There are also what appear to be love songs (though they may be political satires in disguise) and songs of escape from the wearying life of the city and the intrigues of the court to the simple life of the countryside. Some sijo are attributed to the most famous national figures and thinkers of the times. A few are connected with the names of kisaeng. One of these, Hwang Chini, has become a legend for her beauty and her powers of seduction—though the evidence for her existence is suspect—and the small group of poems said to have been composed by her is a set of love songs easily capable of philosophical interpretation. One or two of them are of unusual sensitivity.

Two or three writers of the sixteenth and seventeenth centuries are outstanding, and many critics would accord the palm to Yun Sŏndo as the greatest writer of sijo in Korean history. He sang of the life of the countryside and made moral allegories using symbols from nature which are still fresh and compelling. But before the end of the seventeenth century there were signs of a tendency to deal in conventional fancies rather than produce poetry from experience. It was a troubled period of slow reconstruction after the wars with the Japanese and Manchu invaders, which have been described as the most destructive, cruel, and senseless wars in history. Almost every cultural object above the surface of the ground was destroyed, and the people were impoverished.

Recovery was not complete until the eighteenth century, when Korean culture blossomed again in forms more distinctively native than anything seen in the peninsula since the kings of Silla had deliberately adopted the fashions of T'ang China in the eighth century. It was a renascence centered on an entirely new professional culture. It never became a middle-class culture, because the towns and trade of Korea never developed sufficiently to maintain a bourgeoisie. The culture of the peasants was a folk culture, in which many ancient Korean elements were preserved, but that of the aristocrats was modeled on the life of the palaces in Seoul, heavily influenced by China.

The new professionals were men who belonged to the tiny so-

5

called "middle class" of painters and musicians. They brought some of the vitality of the soil to the service of the arts. They produced Korea's charming animal paintings, with impertinent cats and perky sparrows, as well as frank and satirical pictures of the daily life of ordinary folk, showing tipsy parties on the river, young buddhist monks peering through the bamboos at girls bathing, and the homely occupations of housewives and laborers. Such pictures are peculiarly Korean in concept as well as technique.

Sijo seem to have increased in popularity. It was the time of the compiling of the first anthologies, *Ch'ŏnggu yŏngŏn* ("Chanted Words of the Green Hills"), collected by the singing policeman, Kim Ch'ŏnt'aek, and several others. The songs began to deal more and more with subjects of daily life, and a longer and chattier form, the *sasŏl sijo*, was evolved. Few extant sijo can be traced back to texts earlier than this period, and the great majority of the many anonymous poems seem to have been written from this time onwards.

Where there is no developed practice of criticism, professionalism has its own dangers. Partly because of this, and partly because the expression of the aspirations of the common people posed a threat to the order of society, the nineteenth century marked a decline in the vigor of most Korean arts. In sijo the images became stereotyped—seagulls, peach blossoms, butterflies, bamboos—and elegance, however vapid, came to be more esteemed than content. This is the *hua-niao-feng-yüeh* (flowers and birds, wind and moon) type of verse so despised by the Chinese critics. A few of the best examples use a conceit that rivals the style of the English metaphysical poets, but the majority display a bankrupt reworking of the same old ideas.

It was not until the introduction of western verse forms in the first decade of the twentieth century that the sijo was revivified. Some modern writers have ignored the old sense structure of the sijo (and written amorphous poems as a result), but all have benefited by the influence of western imagery and the consequent broadening of subject matter. Often they lack the lapidary strength of the classic poets, but in their exploration of the pos-

6

sibilities of the changing Korean language they have made good use of the discipline of the sijo form.

Many modern poets feel constricted by the brevity of the sijo, and have continued the old practice of writing cycles of poems. Yun Sŏndo's cycle on the fisherman's year contains forty poems, and Yi Hwang's philosophizing on his rustic retreat runs to twelve. But the older cycles were always truly cycles, in which each poem remained complete in itself. Modern writers often link their sijo in such a way that the individual verses cannot stand alone, and the sijo form becomes merely the stanza pattern for a longer poem.

Do developments such as these stem from a failure to appreciate the true character of the old poems, or do they mark a real step forward in the growth of the sijo tradition? It is too soon to venture an answer; but at least the great volume of poems printed every year in Korea shows that the sijo is still very much alive.

The purpose of this collection is simply to offer to people who do not read Korean some of the pleasure that can be obtained from sijo. The selection is based on whether the poems would be likely to give pleasure in translation; it gives only a limited historical and literary introduction to the genre. Many famous poems have been left out because their understanding and appreciation depend too much on classical Chinese or historical Korean allusions, or because when they are translated the meaning of the poem seems too thin to hold the interest of a foreign reader.

In translating I have tried above all to be faithful to the meaning of the phrases as they seem to be understood by Korean readers. There is a temptation sometimes to translate prettily, echoing, perhaps, the prettiness of countless translations of Japanese verse into English. The result would be loss of the ruggedness which is often characteristic of Korean poems, and the substitution of the delicate vapidity which came to the sijo only in the period of its nineteenth-century decline. I have tried not to tamper with the images, except when too plain a translation might have given a wrong impression.

7

If this "faithful" approach sometimes makes the translations seem flat and prosy, I have happily taken the risk, because the sijo is often colloquial in tone. A dialogue between the poet and the listener is usually presupposed. This is partly because during the period of the classical compositions all writing of importance, even correspondence, was done in Chinese, leaving Korean as the language of spoken communication; and partly because the original poets expected more listeners than readers, for the sijo were intended to be sung.

In addition to the sense I have tried to convey some idea of the poetry's form. I have kept the syllable count exactly in most cases, but I have not adhered rigidly to this rule, partly because a syllable in English often has a very different weight from a syllable in Korean (even in Japanese poetry, which has strict syllable count, it has been found that a slavish adherence to an identical pattern in English translations is undesirable), but also because in sijo, although there is a basic form which can be described in terms of syllable counts, there is considerable variation between one sijo and another. Nevertheless, the translator ought not to ignore special features in the form of each poem. Keeping the original syllable count is a natural way to meet this challenge and a stimulating discipline. Only in the translations of the very diffuse *sasŏl* form have I made no attempt to match the syllables and contented myself with matching the number of phrases.

The play of alliteration and assonance and the placing of the accented syllables are vital to the charm of good sijo. Sometimes the poet's devices are obvious, even naive, and the translator readily hits on a way of expressing them in English. At other times he can spend happy hours trying to devise a solution, only to arrive at a result so contrived that he has betrayed the artlessness of the original. In such situations I have preferred to sacrifice all impression of sound and stay faithful to the meaning. Fortunately in many cases the repetitions of vocabulary required in the English go far to help reproduce the sound pattern of the Korean.

The notes aim to provide sufficient information, without distracting detail, to enable a western reader who has no specialized knowledge of Koreanology to appreciate the songs. Descriptions of the authors include occasional details which may enhance the readers' appreciation of sijo literature as a whole as well as of individual poems. They are given in each case only at the first appearance of the poet's name.

Korean anthologies of sijo have traditionally been organized in several ways: sometimes by approximation to chronological order, sometimes according to the melodies to which the poems are to be sung, or according to subject matter. I have chosen the last way for this collection since it is the most attractive for western readers; but the classification of the songs and subjects is my own. Some of the songs could be placed with equal appropriateness in more than one category, and I have not followed the classification of any one Korean editor.

The original meaning of the word *sijo* is a matter of debate. It is now written with two Chinese characters meaning "time" or "period" and "song," and it has been variously explained as referring to the seasonal significance of the songs or the musical setting appropriate to them. Etymological data are confused. The present use of the word *sijo* seems to date from the 1920's, when Ch'oe Namsŏn first used it in the title of an anthology. Earlier books use *tan'ga* ("short lyric") to describe the words and *sijo* for the tune. The first Westerner to translate sijo was the Canadian James S. Gale, who printed four in the *Korean Repository* in 1894. He called them simply "songs." Before he stopped writing in 1927 he published at least thirty sijo translated from the *Namhun t'aep'yŏng-ga*, but neither he nor others who printed translations in the same period ever called them sijo. Even as late as 1930, when Bishop Trollope's *Corean Books and their Authors* appeared, the word sijo was not used; but sometime after that date the word became generally used to describe the lyrics as well as the tunes, without concern as to its etymological meaning.

The form of sijo is extremely elastic. There are three lines. Each line has a major pause in the middle and a subsidiary pause in the middle of each half-line. The number of syllables in each of the four subsections of a line varies from two to five or more, but the variation which occurs in each part of the poem is different. The possibilities can best be described by two simple tables:

SYLLABLE COUNT OF THE SIJO

(a) *The basic standard:*

First line	3	4	4 (or 3)	4
Middle line	3	4	4 (or 3)	4
Last line	3	5	4	3

(b) *Variants which occur:*

First line	2–5	3–6	2–5	4–6
Middle line	1–5	3–6	2–5	4–6
Last line	3	5–9	4–5	3–4

Each of the three lines is usually less than a complete sentence, and the welding together of the four parts of each line is very close indeed. Often the subsidiary pauses within a line are so weak they almost disappear.

The rhythm of the poem is established by the proportions of the twelve short sections, rather than by tonic accent (as in English) or by syllable count (as in Chinese or Japanese). A rough comparison can be made with the "sprung rhythm" of Gerard Manley Hopkins or the rhythm of Hebrew psalmody, but in sijo it is the phrases that matter, not the accents. The natural accent of Korean is weak, so that the rhythm of poetry cannot be based on a strong metrical beat.

The relative weight of each of the twelve phrases is distributed throughout the poem in such a way as to give the whole poem a proportioned and dynamic shape. In most cases the first and middle lines are completely or very nearly alike in shape and in syllable count. The four phrases of each line may even be all of equal length, but most commonly the first is shorter than the second and the third may be shorter than the fourth. This gives a significant upbeat to the rhythm of these two lines.

The last line has a quite different pattern. The length of the first phrase is invariably fixed at three syllables. In many of the classic poems this is an exclamation or a word of strong emotional value and has a pivotal importance in the structure of the whole poem. The second phrase of the last line is normally the longest in the poem, and in any case must be very syllable-heavy. It draws the last line out slowly in contrast to the first two lines and gives a sense of impending conclusion. The remaining two phrases of the last line are of medium length, but the last phrase of all is merely a grammatical conclusion, both in sense and sound. Since it is frequently cast in a form expressing strong emotional involvement or reaction by the poet, this phrase often intensifies the subjective quality of the poem; but when a sijo is sung it is left out altogether, because it is scarcely necessary for the understanding of the poem and may even detract from its impact on the hearer.

The form of the sijo is normally matched by its sense structure, which is similar to that of a formal Chinese poem of the imitated T'ang type (the kind of Chinese poem most commonly composed in Korea). The theme is stated in the first section; it is developed in the second; an anti-theme or twist is introduced in the third; and the final section is some form of conclusion.

It is interesting to compare this pattern with other verse forms. The Shakespearean sonnet with its three quatrains and couplet, and the T'ang poem with its quatrain formation lend themselves very easily to this fourfold sense structure. The sijo, however, having only three lines in which to deploy the four parts, has to telescope the last two parts into the final line. The effect is most satisfactory. The first line states the theme, and the second, metrically similar, develops it in equal length and power; but the twist at the beginning of the last line acts as a countertheme before the rest of the line completes the poem. The function of the anti-theme is achieved either by loading the twist phrase emotionally, as happens when it is composed of a single exclamatory word, or by introducing a word or idea that is in sharp contrast to the tone of the first two lines.

When the twist is produced by a change in the imagery the feeling of abrupt change can often be missed in translation because the traditional association of images in groups that was part of the mental furniture of old oriental poets is lacking from our own literary sensitivities. The Korean boy began his study with a series of Chinese primers which teach the elements of a cosmogony in which the various planes of existence are arranged in parallel categories. The spring season goes with the element wood, the color blue—which Orientals, like the Greeks, did not distinguish from green—the eastern point of the compass, the dragon among the beasts, the plum blossom among plants, and so on. Summer goes with fire, red, the south, the divine phoenix (really a mythical peacock or pheasant), the peony and the orchid, and so forth. A change from any one of these categories to another would strike traditional Orientals with a force which a modern Westerner would not easily sense, and this type of change would be a most effective anti-theme in a sijo.

The conclusion of a sijo is seldom epigrammatic or witty. A witty close to a sentence would have been foreign to the genius of stylized Korean diction in the great sijo periods. As has already been noted, the grammatical ending of a sentence is weak in image power and not necessary to the hearer for him to grasp the sense of the poem. A sijo in translation may therefore often seem to lack the firm clinch that the Westerner would expect in a poem whose style and length suggest an epigram. Korean epigrammatic utterance must be sought in the homely field of proverb; the sijo is essentially aristocratic, and remained so until the awakening of a culture among the lower classes in the eighteenth century. Thus a sijo may sometimes seem vague to the Westerner and almost incomplete, but it always has an explicit statement of the poet's concern. The three long lines give the poet plenty of room to express himself, more like a Chinese quatrain than the very brief Japanese haiku which by its smallness forces the poet merely to suggest his meaning.

In spite of the fact that the sijo is a purely Korean form, the tone, subject matter, and language of many old sijo are heavily impregnated with Chinese words and ideas. This fact does not in the least detract from the genuine Koreanness of the songs. Chinese influence was of dominating importance in sophisticated Korean culture from the eighth to the nineteenth centuries. Proper names, almost without exception, were Chinese. This fact apart, the parallel with the role of the classical cultures of Greece and Rome in medieval and modern European culture is striking. Just as Shakespeare drew his imagery more readily from the mythology of the Mediterranean area than from the northern tradition, so the Korean scholar, steeped in the literature of China, drew his literary examples and similes from Chinese sources.

The extensive Chinese background of sijo imagery is merely a part of the typical Korean thought of the period. Chinese names are frequently used, and the treatment of birds, flowers, mythical beasts, and indeed the whole of nature derives ultimately from Chinese tradition. So deeply steeped were all educated Koreans in Chinese literature that the whole thought of many old sijo is a perfect reflection of the thought of the T'ang poets. This is especially true of the songs about nature and about farewells, but other poems, too, are closely dependent on the entirely Chinese literary milieu from which they emerged.

In some cases there is an unmistakable Korean flavor to the treatment of this Chinese material. Some poets, such as Chŏng Ch'ŏl, develop the tradition in their own distinctive way. But even when they do not, it is unwise to characterize the Korean poets as being merely derivative. Not only should the parallel with European renascence culture be borne in mind, but the oriental attitude to what the West calls plagiarism must be understood. Imitation of previous good writing, extensive and aesthetically apt quotation, subtle changing of well-known texts to create slightly new effects, and other such devices were not despised in the Orient. Rather were they admired, and, especially in Japan, sometimes carried to extreme lengths. Standards of modern criticism which have grown up partly in a world of copyrights and competitive publishing do not apply to traditional oriental literature. Again, it is worth remembering that Shakespeare borrowed most of his plots from other men's books, and even today no one thinks the worse of him for having done so.

The parallel between the role of Chinese thought in Korean

culture and of Latin or Greek thought in English culture can be extended to apply to the language itself. Korean still retains a vast vocabulary of Chinese-derived words, and they all can be written with Chinese logograms as well as with Korean script according the current Korean pronunciation (which preserves many phonetic features of the Chinese language of T'ang and Sung times.) Some of these words (like the Latin words absorbed into the English language by Anglo-Saxon monks) have become so naturalized that they represent ideas for which there is no native word, but the majority of them are to some degree literary. The effect they have in composition can reasonably be compared to the effect of a latinate vocabulary in English. In Augustan poetry it is fine; in official letters it can become gobbledygook.

This use of Chinese in literary Korean allows whole phrases to be incorporated without alteration of their original Chinese grammar. In some sijo this is carried to extreme lengths when a complete verse or couplet, or even a whole quatrain, may be inserted into the body of the Korean poem. Examples can be found in this book in Nos. 5, 23, 55, 96, 201, and 243. However, it is much more commonplace for phrases of three to six Chinese characters to be grafted into the Korean sentences, and this is what happens in the majority of the old sijo.

Although used instinctively by the poets, this technique produces a peculiar quality, enriching and enhancing the beauty of the songs. In modern writing, as the influence of Chinese culture in Korea steadily wanes, the practice is disappearing, and what was highly esteemed in the past is nowadays often not fully appreciated.

An examination of a classic sijo will clarify the description of its form. This is a poem attributed to Sŏng Sammun (1418–1456), a great loyalist who was put to death by a usurping king for attempting to replace the ousted boy king Tanjong on the throne. It is an imitation of another famous sijo of loyalty attributed to a much earlier figure, Chŏng Mongju (1337–1392), and this echo must have originally increased the poem's impact.

The three lines of the original are here shown as six for typographical convenience. The syllable count is the same as in the Korean original. An alternative version is appended for the last line.

(1) When this frame   is dead and gone
     what will then   become of me?
(2) On the peak   of Pongnae-san
     I shall become   a spreading pine.
(3) When white snow   fills heaven and earth
     I shall still stand   lone and green.
or: I'll stay, lone, green   (will I stay).

The first line states the theme as a question—a common device which enables the development in the second line to be worked out very simply as an answer to the question. In this case the answer involves the name of the traditional oriental fairyland, Pongnae (Chinese *P'eng-lai-shan*) or the Islands of the Blessed in the Eastern Ocean, a most appropriate place for a man's soul after death. The same name is also given to the famous and spectacular Diamond Mountains of Korea in summer because the meaning of Pongnae-san suggests abundant foliage. (The Chŏng Mongju poem used the winter name of the Diamond Mountains in a similar way.) The use of "white snow" at the beginning of the last line is, therefore a dramatic change from the category of summer images to that of winter hardship, while the final pine-tree image, though appropriate to winter (as an evergreen), retains the tree imagery implied in the name of Pongnae-san.

In the two translations of the last half-line, the upper version makes the more readable English but the lower indicates more clearly the effect of the Korean grammar: the last phrase, adding nothing to the imagery, can be omitted with no loss to the sense.

Metrically the syllable scheme is nearly ideal and shows the essential pattern and movement of the sijo form to good advantage.

The translation does not represent the word music of the original:

                 i momi chugŏ kasŏ
                         muŏsi toelko hani
                 Pongnae-san cheil bonge
                         nangnakchangsong toeŏttaga
                 paeksŏri man'gŏn'gonhal che
                         togyach'ŏngch'ŏng harira

In Korean the opening question is highly rhythmic, but is composed entirely of native Korean words, any one of which might occur in daily conversation in Korea during the past five centuries. The effect is light and easy. The answer, beginning in the middle line, is in a different mode, composed almost entirely of borrowed Chinese words, which are more sonorous and heavy. The last line is almost completely Chinese in grammar as well as in vocabulary, and has a dramatic solemnity quite at variance with the conversational style of the opening but forming a perfect conclusion to it.

There are obvious sound patterns in the middle and last lines: alliteration and playing on the long *a* sound in the phrase "spreading pine"; repetition of the final *n* in the phrase "fills heaven and earth" and a final duplication of the strong sound of *ch'ŏngch'ŏng* (green, so green).

The total effect is disciplined, but no suspicion of contrivance remains. It makes a statement which is clear enough grammatically, but which is essentially symbolic, based on the oriental cliché of the pine tree as a symbol of the upright heart. The subject of the poem is not, as the western reader might suppose, a declaration of belief in immortality, but a protestation of loyalty, a declaration that the poet's steadfastness will be remembered forever as an inspiring example. It is quite probable that Sŏng Sammun believed in some form of life after death, but this poem has no bearing on that matter.

If tradition is right in believing that this poem was composed with reference to Sŏng's political martyrdom, it is in yet another sense a superb example of the genre. But sijo are often difficult to interpret.

In many of the better examples of sijo it is possible to analyze the way in which the poet has orchestrated his sounds so as to give the poem an aural pattern which often conforms to the general outline of the sense structure. This is a natural device for a sensitive speaker of Korean, because the Korean language has strong traces of "vowel harmony" in its grammar, and there are no heavy clusters of consonants such as are typical of English. (To pronounce a phrase like "primrose paths to glory" a Korean is tempted to insert six extra vowels to break up the converging consonant sounds.)

It is easy to speak of alliteration and assonance in describing sijo, but the use of sounds is actually more complex than these two terms suggest. It is not even strictly speaking a matter of "head rhyme." It is rather the composition of similar types of sounds, both vowels and consonants, into harmonious patterns of a simpler and more striking nature than we are used to in English.

In the following romanized version of the poem attributed to Admiral Yi Sunsin, the consonants should be pronounced approximately as in English and the vowels as in Italian. There is a slight tonic stress on the first syllable of each word group.

Hansansŏm tal palgŭn pame, suru-e honja anja
        K'ŭn k'al yŏp'e ch'ago, kip'ŭn sirŭm h'anŭn ch'a-e
Ŏdisŏ ilsŏng-hoganŭn, nae-ŭi aerŭl gŭnnani?

> By moonlight I sit all alone
> > in the lookout on Hansan isle.
> My sword is on my thigh,
> > I am submerged in deep despair.
> From somewhere the shrill note of a pipe:
> > will it sever my heartstrings?

In the first line the sound *a* is the dominant vowel, and is taken up again at the end of the line in the nearly rhyming *honja anja*. The chief consonant sounds are the liquids *l*, *m*, and *n*. The result is a very smooth-sounding line, setting the peaceful scene where the poet is sitting alone in a tower on an island in the moonlight.

The romanization of the middle line happily shows how full it is of aspirated sounds, which break harshly on the ear after the gentle first line. The martial strength and determination symbolized by the great sword, and the bitterness of the commander's worries and sorrows are forcefully represented by this abrupt change of sound. The effect is enhanced by the high-pitched sound of the *i* vowel—the sound furthest away from the smooth *a* and *o*—which does not occur in the poem until the words for "deep sorrow," *kip'ŭn sirŭm*. The middle line has developed the theme of the first line, and the development has been subtly contrived by carrying the vowel harmony of the first line through the first half of the middle line, while at the same time modulating to a new consonant pattern of strong aspirates.

The last line begins with the three-syllable "twist phrase," *ŏdisŏ*, meaning "from somewhere," a change of sense managed by directing the attention away from the tower and the poet. The next phrase, *ilsŏng-hoganŭn*, is a Chinese locution meaning "a single pipe note." Such Chinese phrases have a singularly orotund effect when inserted into a Korean sentence. They seem to comprise much in little, because to express the same meaning in pure Korean words would take more syllables, and so they have something of the conciseness that Latin phrases used to have for cultivated English ears. In addition they often have a marked emotional value, because they are frequently familiar or allusive. In this case the length of the vowels gives the phrase a heavy sound, heralding the end of the poem.

The final phrase, "will it sever my heartstrings?", is filled with indistinct vowels and liquid consonants (*n, r,* and *l*), which would have trailed off to a whimper had not the hard *g* of *gŭnnani* cut into it like a knife cutting a cord.

One of the later anonymous sijo illustrates the same features of Korean poetry, and in addition provides examples of Korean word play:

Subak-kŏtch'i duryŏt-han nima, ch'amwi-gŏt'ŭn malsŭm maso.
Kaji-kaji hasinŭn mari, malmada oen mariroda.
Kusiwŏl psidonga kŏtch'i sok sŏnggin mal marŭsiso.

Beloved, you're smooth as a watermelon,
        but don't use honeydew words to me.
Your words come thick as aubergines,
        but they are crooked as gherkins.
Give up your hollow talk,
        empty as candied gourds in autumn.

The first line ("Beloved, you're smooth as a watermelon, but don't use honeydew words to me") is composed of two parallel phrases, each of which concludes with a group of syllables in which nasal sounds and *a* sounds are dominant. The tone and theme are established by two bantering similes, which are balanced in sound as well as in meaning.

The second line develops the sense with two puns. The obvious meaning of the line is "Everything you say is all lies"; but the phrase *kaji-kaji*, besides being a duplication of the ordinary word for "thing"—making a colloquial plural "everything"—is also a pun on the word *kaji*, meaning aubergine or eggplant. And the word *oen*, meaning "false," is also a pun on the word *oe* (with a grammatical suffix *n*), meaning a cucumber or gherkin. The sense is clear, but the theme of similes with gourds or melonlike fruits is carried over from the first line by the puns. (In translation one must either ignore the pun or turn it into simile.)

The sounds of the second line are characterized by the predominance of the *a* vowel. In the first half of the line it alternates with the *i* sound in a mocking jingle, and that combination is echoed again in the last "foot." The last half of the line is smoothed with nasal and liquid sounds, variegated by two well-placed *d*'s. (It should be noted that in Korean *r* and *l* belong to one phoneme, and so are emotionally regarded as the same sound.)

The third line begins with a word meaning "September and October." Leaving the ideas of talking and vegetables for a moment, the "twist" of a time phrase has been introduced. This is not only one of the concise Chinese phrases; it also has a blend of sounds that have not previously appeared in the poem. All three of its vowels are, by Korean reckoning, "feminine" (*yin*) or "cloudy," as opposed to the "masculine" (*yang*) or "clear" sounds of *o* and *a* that have been so much used in the previous lines.

The next phrase, *psidonga kotch'i*, resumes the similes of the opening line. It refers to a kind of white melon which when preserved will produce its own natural sugar; but it is then dry, and the withered inner pith is removed. The beloved's words are not to be empty like such a melon. The final verb *marŭsiso* echoes the end of the first line *maso* and has a similar meaning. The vowel sounds are mingled much as the sounds of the first line are, but the sibilants are heard more strongly than before. The *ps* of *psidonga* is very strong, and so is the middle sound of *sok sŏnggin* ("empty inside"). The six hissing *s* sounds make the last line come out like a spit or snarl.

Altogether it is a most satisfying poem, deceptive in its apparent artlessness but in fact delightfully constructed, with the sense subtly supported by the play of the sounds, and all bound together by the vegetable theme expressed half in simile and half in puns.

One of the best known of moralizing sijo is the mountain-climbing allegory of Yang Saŏn. It has a curiously Victorian ring, and for that reason I am not at all sure that the following translation is not to be preferred to my own. This translation was made by a Methodist missionary some twenty years ago. It seems that he did not write it down, but it was memorized by a Canadian missionary who recited it to me. He could not remember the Methodist's name.

> Men may say the mountain's high,
> >   but all of it's beneath the sky;
> There really is no reason why
> >   we may not climb if we climb and climb,
> But usually we never try.
> >   We only say: "The mountain's high."

The Korean text is:

T'aesani nopta hadoe, hanŭrarae moeiroda.
Orŭgo ddo orŭmyŏn, mot orŭlli ŏpkŏnmanŭn
Sarami che ani orŭgo, moerŭl nopta hanani?

With interlinear word-for-word translation:

T'aesani	nopta	hadoe
T'aishan	is high	they say, yet

	hanŭrarae	moeiroda
	under the sky	it is a mountain.

Orŭgo ddo orŭmyŏn
Climbing and climbing (if one does)

	mot orŭlli	ŏpkŏnmanŭm
	cannot climb	is not the case

Sarami	che	ani	orŭgo
Man	himself	not	climbing

	moerŭl	nopta	hanani?
	mountains	high	does he say?

The preponderance of *a* and *o* sounds is striking. Palatalized vowels (i.e., with a *y* sound in front of them) are almost entirely absent, and there is no single occurrence of a rounded *u* at any point. Drawing a strained metaphor from music, one might say that the effect is of unison rather than harmony. The pattern of the vowels is almost monotonously homogenous. Only the presence of the scattered *i* sounds lends interest to the aural impact. The effect is enhanced by the lack of harsh consonants. Only the initial *T'* is aspirated (the *h* sounds in Korean are comparatively weak between vowels). The only glottalized hard consonant is in the *ddo* of the second line. The whole poem flows smoothly along with a collection of "clear" or "masculine" vowels and soft consonants. And this uniformity of sound is reinforced by the use of the same verb (*orŭ*, to climb) four times over.

The thought has a corresponding simplicity. Three nouns (mountain, sky, man), one verb (to climb), and only one adjective (high) are the sum total of the Korean lexical material. The rest is grammatical suffixes. This is extreme economy.

The opening phrase uses the name of a Chinese mountain, T'aishan, which has become typical of all high mountains—it means, quite simply, "High Mountain." The second phrase qualifies the height of the great mountain and sets the didactic tone. It contains four crisp dental sounds (*t* and *d*).

The second line has a dental sound near the beginning, but a duplicated and strong one, indicating the effort involved in persevering; the repetitive use of the verb and the long *o* sound contribute to the same idea. The theme of height is developed into the idea of climbing.

The last line makes the twist by injecting the idea of man. It could be "mankind" or "a man." Before this, the poem has not mentioned humanity except by implication. The explicit reference to man at this point shows that the clinching of the moral argument is imminent. The immediate use of *che* (himself) is impressive: it is the only palatal consonant in the poem, and the vowel *e* does not occur elsewhere (the *oe* sound is notably different). But the return to the verb *orŭgo* (climbing) binds the new phrase to the previous one, and the final question uses material from the phrase at the beginning of the poem. It is a neat rounding off.

Such sijo seem effortless. It is claiming too much to suggest that in every good example the poet was consciously exercising his craftsmanship, because there is no tradition of criticism of sijo writing technique comparable to the highly analytical tradition of poetic craftsmanship in Chinese. Nevertheless, the best sijo derive their compelling charm from the organization of the phonetic resources and peculiarities of the Korean language in a way which can be analyzed. Korean critics have not yet begun to investigate this aspect of sijo, but a study of it greatly enhances one's appreciation of the songs. And it is in this quality that the translation-defying thisness of each sijo ultimately resides.

The Songs

Historical Songs

1

The white snow has left the valleys
      where the clouds are lowering.
Is it true that somewhere
      the plum trees have happily blossomed?
I stand here alone in the dusk
      and do not know where to go.

YI SAEK (1328–1396)

The poet, a distinguished confucian scholar-official, remained loyal to
the Koryŏ dynasty during the stormy period in which it succumbed to
the rising Yi family. The surname Yi means "plum tree."

2

Fate is full of ups and downs:
      here's autumn hay on Manwŏltae,
The herdboy's pipes are heard
      where kings ruled for five centuries.
If I come here in the evening,
      I cannot restrain my tears.

WŎN CH'ŎNSŎK (late 14th century)

After the fall of Koryŏ and the removal of the capital to Seoul a faith-
ful courtier of the old dynasty revisits Manwŏltae (Full Moon Terrace)
in the derelict city of Songdo, which had been renamed Kaesŏng.
    Wŏn left the court when the dynasty changed and went to live with
his parents as a farmer in central Korea. When he died he left six sealed
volumes of writings, forbidding his sons to open them. They disobeyed
him and discovered he had written an account of the end of Koryŏ
which was so compromising that they burned the books.

3

The north wind moans amid the bare boughs,

        the moon shines coldly on the snow.

I stand, great sword in hand,

        on the furthest frontier fortress.

I whistle; and the long loud sound

        hangs unanswered on the air.

KIM CHONGSŎ (1390–1453)

The poet distinguished himself by gaining territory on the Manchurian border during the reign of Sejong, the king who invented the Korean alphabet. He was also an annalist and scholar. In a later reign he and his two sons were assassinated by supporters of Prince Suyang, who was then aiming to wrest the throne from the boy king, Tanjong.

4

Idling beneath the thatched roof,

        pillowing my head on my lute,

I wanted to dream

        of the great king's reign of peace.

At the gate a fisherman's pipe

        trills a few notes and wakes me.

YU SŎNGWŎN (d. 1456)

The great king who reigned in peace was Sejong, still the most gratefully remembered of Korean rulers. The few notes are said to be the news of the assassination of Kim Chongsŏ by order of Prince Suyang, who later usurped the throne from the boy king Tanjong and is now known as King Sejo. The poet was one of the famous Six Martyred Subjects of Tanjong, men who died in an attempt to restore Tanjong to the throne.

He had earlier been one of the group of scholars who worked with King Sejong on the invention of the alphabet.

5

The cuckoo calls, the moon hangs low on the mountains.
        I am longing and lonely, leaning on this parapet.
You cry mournfully; and my heart is weary:
        if you did not call, I should not be sad.
Go, tell man he is a parting guest:
        let him not come here in spring when the cuckoo
        calls, and the moonlight silvers the pavilion!

        KING TANJONG (1441–1457)

This poem is said to have been written by Tanjong after he was exiled by his uncle, Prince Suyang, to the mountains of Yŏngwŏl in Kang-wŏn-do, and shortly before he was assassinated.

The meter is not regular sijo meter, and the language is almost entirely Chinese. The pavilion where the poem is said to have been composed still stands in Yŏngwŏl town.

The use of the cuckoo as a symbol of sorrow is typical. (cf. No. 126)

6

Ten thousand *li* along the road
        I bade farewell to my fair young lord.
My heart can find no rest
        as I sit beside a stream.
That water is like my soul:
        it goes sighing into the night.

        WANG PANGYŎN (15th century)

Wang had accompanied the boy Tanjong to his exile. Later he went with the royal messenger who took the hemlock for Tanjong to drink—following the custom that condemned royalty were bound to commit suicide by drinking poison.

"Ten thousand *li*" is a deliberate exaggeration. A distance of ten *li* is an hour's walk.

That candle burning indoors,
>>> to whom has it bidden farewell?
While its outside drips with tears,
>>> does it not know that its heart burns?
I also, my King left a thousand leagues back,
>>> I burn inside and I weep.

>>> YI KAE (1417–1456)

Yi Kae was another of the Six Martyred Subjects. This poem refers to Tanjong's banishment, and is based on a poem by the T'ang poet Tu Mu.

8

So they say there was a gale
>>> and frosty snow fell last night?
And the spreading pines were
>>> all broken and overthrown?
In that case how about the flowers,
>>> what chance have they to blossom?

>>> YU ŬNGBU (d. 1456)

Yu Ŭngbu was another of the Six Martyred Subjects in the Tanjong affair. He was a huge and serious man, of great courage. It is said that when he was being tortured and the branding irons cooled off a little, he told the executioners to reheat them. But he was equally famous for his lifelong devotion to his mother.

The pines are the loyal men of high rank, the flowers are the younger men of lower rank; but the song has also been interpreted as a reflection of the hopelessness of the times, bewailing the lot of the common people.

9

By moonlight I sit all alone
           in the lookout on Hansan isle.
My sword is on my thigh,
           I am submerged in deep despair.
From somewhere the shrill note of a pipe . . .
           will it sever my heartstrings?

YI SUNSIN (1545–1599)

Supposedly written by the great admiral who saved Korea from the Japanese by his invention and management of the famous armor-clad "turtle-ships." It has been suggested that this poem is an elegy for his friend who died in the battle of Pusan, but Korean commentators usually interpret it as expressing the anxiety of a commander-in-chief. The diction of this poem is discussed in the Introduction, and its literary history in the note on Texts and Sources.

10

The spring mountain is ablaze,
           unopened buds are burning.
Water could quench
           that mountain fire.
But in me a smokeless fire is raging
           that no water can put out.

KIM TŎNGNYŎNG (1567–1596)

The poet was a courageous leader against the Japanese invaders, but he was arrested on a false charge of treason and sent to prison, where he died. The poem is said to have been written while he was in prison, when he was twenty-eight years old.

11

Blue Serpent sword on my shoulder
    I ride on a pure white deer,
Flying over hills and waters
    to the mystic Mulberry Tree.
The clear sound of bronze bells and jade chimes
    rings from the fairy palace through the clouds.

    KO KYŎNGMYŎNG (1533–1592)

Ko Kyŏngmyŏng met his death while leading levies against the invading armies of Hideyoshi. The mystic mulberry tree in Chinese legend is the place in the eastern sea whence the sun rises. (Since the Korean word for mulberry is *bong*, it is hard to resist the conclusion that this was also the place where the owl and the pussycat eventually got married.)

The poem uses Taoist symbols to suggest superhuman determination. The sounds from beyond the sky may be summonses of immortality—the soldier poet is prepared to die in battle. But some commentators prefer to interpret the song as a yearning for sequestered life and contemplative ecstasy. This was probably the original intention.

12

The rain that pits the clear stream,
    what has it got to laugh about?
Mountain leaves and flowers,
    why do they shake with joyous mirth?
They are right. Spring does not last many days.
    While we can laugh, laugh away.

    KING HYOJONG (1619–1659)

In 1636 the Manchu invaded and subjugated Korea. The poet, who was then the Prince Pongnim, was sent with the crown prince as a hostage to the Manchu court at Peking, where he remained for eight years. This poem is said to be one of several that he wrote in the course of the journey to China.

For the last ten years of his life the prince ruled Korea. His posthumous title is Hyojong.

Political Songs

13

Pine-tree rising beside the road,
        what is it makes you stand there?
Relax for a little while
        and stand down into the ditch:
Every rope-girded peasant that carries an axe
        will want to cut you down.

CHŎNG CH'ŎL (1536–1593)

A moral warning to those who like prominent posts, from one of Korea's greatest poets. He had a checkered career, always in and out of office. When he was out of office he was usually in exile in the countryside. He was deeply involved in factional struggles, but his intransigent uprightness did not make his path in politics any smoother.

14

Did I hear those boats have gone
        that late were bobbing in the waves?
As soon as the clouds gathered
        were they forced to disappear?
All of you whose boats are leaky
        heed the warning and take care.

CHŎNG CH'ŎL (1536–1593)

A warning for would-be politicians and seekers of high office, drawing again on the poet's own disillusioning experiences.

15

Can tiny insects

        devour a whole great spreading pine?

Where is the long-billed

        woodpecker? Why is he not here?

When I hear the sound of falling trees

        I cannot contain myself for sorrow.

    ANONYMOUS

An allegory of political life. The Korean court during most of the Yi dynasty was the scene of continual jostling for power. Frequent impeachment of ministers, often on trivial ceremonial issues, deprived the country of stable leadership—symbolized here by the woodpecker who is needed to destroy the insects.

16

White gull skimming

        over the water—

Somebody happened to spit

        and the spittle hit the gull's back.

White seagull! Do not be angry:

        the world, you know, is messy.

    CHŎNG CH'ŎL (1536–1593)

The phrase used for "water" (literally "rivers and lakes") is a classical locution meaning a place of retirement and meditation.

17

Huge beams and rooftree timbers
           are rejected and thrown away;
While the house is falling down
           they argue with one another.
Carpenters, when will you stop
           running around with your ink-cups and rules?

CHŎNG CH'ŎL (1536–1593)

Oriental carpenters use a small cup of Chinese ink with a thread for marking timbers. The thread runs through the ink and is then held taut over the wood to produce a straight line.

This poem may refer to the preoccupation of Korean statesmen with minor domestic issues during the period when the country was threatened by the ambition of Japan. Hideyoshi's invasion took place at the very end of Chŏng Ch'ŏl's lifetime.

18

Peach and plum of springtime
           do not flaunt your pretty blossoms;
Consider rather the old pine
           and green bamboo at year's end.
What can change these noble stems
           and their flourishing evergreen?

KIM YUGI (late 17th century)

Kim Yugi was a famous singer at the court of King Sukchong and a close friend of Kim Ch'ŏnt'aek (see No. 27).

The opening phrase is quoted from the *Ch'ang-hen-ko* of Po Chü-i, but derives from the *Book of Songs*, and suggests the beauty of young women.

19

A boatman troubled by the storms
　　　　sold his boat and bought a pony,
But found the twisting paths
　　　　were more alarming than the waves.
Now maybe, leaving both boat and pony
　　　　he'll start simply ploughing fields.

CHANG MAN (1566–1629)

The poet had a checkered political career during a period when Korea was suffering coups d'état and rebellions. He rose to the rank of county prefect during the reign of the profligate tyrant Kwanghae-gun, but foresaw the collapse of the king and withdrew to his ancestral home. During the following reign he returned to office and earned merit for his work in quelling the rebellion of Yi Kwal. In the Manchu war of 1627 he was exiled in disgrace, only to be recalled later, and finally given the supreme accolade of a posthumous honorific name.

Ploughing is done with oxen, not with ponies or horses.

20

I was bent by the wind.
　　　　Do not deride a twisted pine:
Can the flowers of spring
　　　　always keep their prettiness?
Howling winds and swirling snow will come,
　　　　and then you will envy me.

PRINCE INP'YŎNG (1622–1658)

After the Ch'ing ascendancy and subjection of Korea Prince Inp'yŏng was often sent on embassies to the Chinese court. He wrote several poems referring to the shame of Korea's defeat by the Ch'ing forces. His Chinese calligraphy is highly esteemed.

Drinking Songs

21

The boys have gone to dig bracken,
   the bamboo grove is empty now.
Who will tidy up
   the scattered chessmen and board?
Drunken I lie on a pine tree root,
   and don't know whether day has dawned.

CHŎNG CH'ŎL (1536–1593)

22

The moon is swollen full,
   suspended in a jade sky.
It might so easily
   fall down in the frosty winds of time.
But just now I want it to shine
   on my tipsy guest's golden cup.

YI TŎKHYŎNG (1561–1613)

Yi Tŏkhyŏng was a chief minister of state who won renown in the invasion of Korea by Hideyoshi. At the age of thirty-one he had been Minister of Rites and Rector of the National Confucian College (Sŏng-gyun-gwan), but he was finally ousted by factional strife and died while exiled in the countryside.

23

Although the last snow had melted
>I did not know that spring was here.

"Migrating geese are urged through clearing skies,
>Dormant willows come to life above the
rippling waters"—

Here, my boy, bring a cup and drink with me:
>we must welcome the spring anew.

KIM SUJANG (1690– ?)

The middle section (within the quotation marks) is a Chinese couplet quoted verbatim and pressed into the sijo form.

Kim Sujang has left more sijo than any other writer. He was a friend of Kim Ch'ŏnt'aek, and like him a minor official. In 1763, when he was very old indeed, he compiled the famous anthology of sijo called *Haedong kayo* ("Songs from Beyond the Eastern Sea," "Beyond Eastern Sea" being a classic sobriquet for Korea).

24

When flowers bloom, I think of the moon;
>when the moon shines, my thoughts turn to wine.

When flowers bloom in the moonlight,
>if I have wine, then I want a friend.

Dare I hope to have a friend beneath the blossom
>drinking in both moonlight and flowers?

YI CHŎNGBO (1693–1766)

Yi Chŏngbo had a distinguished career in government in an age of relative peace and prosperity. In old age he retired to the country, and possibly then wrote some of his many poems, both in Chinese and in Korean.

25

Tucking away the plectrum of my lute
    I slip into a quiet noonday nap,
But the dog at the gate
    barks to announce a welcome friend.
Hurry, boy! Get some lunch ready quickly,
    but first go strain some fresh wine.

KIM CH'ANGŎP (1658–1721)

Kim Ch'angŏp was the son and brother of prime ministers, but had no taste for politics, preferring to remain in the countryside as a farmer. When his brother was banished from court he went with him and died in exile.

26

Yesterday I was dead drunk,
    and today it's wine again.
Was I sober the day before yesterday?
    The day before that I cannot recall.
Tomorrow I have asked a friend to West Lake:
    Shall I be sober—perhaps?

PRINCE YUCH'ŎN (17th century)

Prince Yuch'ŏn, a great-grandson of King Sŏnjo, was famous as a painter and calligrapher.

West Lake was a poetic name for the modern Sŏgang, near Seoul, imitated from a famous resort near Hang-chou in China.

27

I shed my coat and told the boy

        to pawn it at a wine shop.

Now I look up at the sky,

        I address the moon, and say:

Well now! What about old Li Po?

        How would he compare with me?

        KIM CH'ŎNT'AEK (18th century)

Li Po was the notorious drinker and pre-eminent poet of T'ang China who found a hundred poems in a single cup of wine. This sijo is based on the closing lines of his poem *Chiang-chin-chiu*.

    Kim Ch'ŏnt'aek was a prolific writer of sijo and a famous singer. He has left only slightly fewer songs than his close friend Kim Sujang. In 1728 he edited the first of the great sijo anthologies, *Ch'ŏnggu yŏngŏn* ("Korean Songs").

28

A million waves of sea

        could not wash away my thousand cares,

But just one bottle of wine

        has cleansed them all this very day.

In this way Li Po of old

        slept long hours, worry-free.

        ANONYMOUS

This poem also incorporates phrases quoted from Li Po.

29

How did Li Po drink so much wine as he did—
> at least three hundred cups a day?
And how did Tu Mu-chih reach that state of bliss,
> pulling a cartload of oranges
> through Yang-chou?
I doubt if I can ever hope
> to reach the level of Li and Tu.

ANONYMOUS

Tu Mu-chih (Tu Mu), like Li Po, was not only a notorious drinker but also one of the greatest poets of T'ang China and as such greatly admired in Korea.

30

Drowsy with wine in the twilight
> and slumped on the back of a donkey.
Ten leagues of hills and streams
> were passed as in a dream.
Suddenly I am awakened
> by the notes of a fisherman's pipe.

CHO CHUN (d. 1405)

Cho Chun was one of the ministers who helped in the founding of the Yi dynasty from 1392 onwards.

Moral Songs

31

White egret, do not laugh at
        the raven for being black
He may be black outside;
        does that mean he's black inside?
And perhaps snow-white plumage can conceal
        a black heart. Could that be you?

YI CHIK (1362–1431)

The author, a great-grandson of the poet Yi Chŏnyŏn, was one of the supporters of the rising Yi dynasty, and became prime minister. The poem is taken by some commentators to be an expression of a troubled conscience—he ought to have remained faithful to the Koryŏ dynasty. But it is easy for later generations to read such meanings back into these poems.

32

A grub can become a cicada,
        spread its wings and fly away.
On the tallest of tall trees
        it can sing its finest song.
But up there spiders spin their webs:
        it behoves you to be wary of them.

ANONYMOUS

33

Though they say, "The hills are high,"
        all hills are still below heaven.
By climbing, climbing, climbing more,
        there is no peak cannot be scaled.
But the man who never tried to climb,
        he says indeed: "The hills are high."

YANG SAŎN (1517–1584)

The poet was a local government official who delighted in visiting the Diamond Mountains. No other sijo remains from his hand, but this is one of the most widely known of old Korean poems. It is discussed in the Introduction, where another translation is also given.

34

When man and wife are wed,
        it is a precious union.
"He calls, she comes," they say;
        thus heaven and earth keep harmony.
Like Meng-kuang with the tray to her eyebrows,
        wives should revere their husbands.

PAK INNO (1561–1642)

One of a cycle of poems on the five cardinal relationships of confucianism. "He calls, she comes," is a quotation from the *Ch'ien-tzŭ-wen* or "Thousand Character Classic," the book that was traditionally used by Korean boys as a primer of Chinese characters. Meng-kuang was a famous wife of ancient China who revered her husband so much that when she served him his daily meals "she never presumed to stare up into his eyes but held up the serving table level with her eyebrows." This poem is typical of Pak Inno's didacticism.

Pak spent much of his active life in naval service, but retired at the age of fifty. In spite of his heavy reliance on Chinese allusion he is highly esteemed by Korean literary historians.

35

What is black, they say is white,

   what is white they say is black.

Be it white, be it black,

   nobody says that I am right.

I had best stop my ears, close my eyes,

   and refuse to judge things.

  KIM SUJANG (1690– ?)

36

Benevolence is the house site,

   respect and loyalty the pillars.

If all is cemented

   with modesty and courtesy,

Though there come ten million years of storms,

   can there be fear of falling?

  CHU ŬISIK (18th century)

Chu was remembered as a gentle and quiet man who was skilled at making brush drawings of plum blossom. The sentiments of this song are of purest Confucian orthodoxy.

37

Ten years have passed since I last saw
>the white jade cup in the Office of Books.

Its pale, clear color
>stays exactly as it was before.

How is it that a man's heart
>changes from morning to night?

CHŎNG CH'ŎL (1536–1593)

The Office of Books (Chungsŏ-dang or Hongmun-gwan) was charged with the care of the confucian classic texts and the drafting of royal decrees. The same office is referred to as the Jade Hall in No. 59.

38

A muddy piece of jade
>cast away beside the road . . .

Those who come and go here
>must think it's nothing but dirt.

But maybe someone will know better.
>Stay put there: look like earth.

YUN TUSŎ (18th century)

Yun Tusŏ was the son of the more famous poet Yun Sŏndo. He gives to the proverbial "Little gems are where you find them" an ascetic twist which echoes the preference of the best of his class of men for uprightness of character and retired manner of life.

Let's strain off raw rice wine
    and drink till our lips are shrunk;
Let's simmer our bitter herbs
    and chew them till they taste sweet,
Walk on till our thick studded clogs
    are worn to their wooden soles.

CHŎNG CHʼŎL (1536–1593)

This song is regarded as an exhortation to complete anything which is undertaken, and also to make the most of frugal circumstances. Raw wine, bitter herbs, and wooden clogs are not the finest products, but they are to be used for all they are worth. Chŏng Chʼŏl wrote dull didactic poems, but here proves that he could transform even that genre.

You sparrows, all chittering
    after sun has set and day is over,
Even half a branch
    has room for all your tiny bodies.
Why must you be so jealous
    when you have a whole thicket to roost in?

ANONYMOUS

41

Fresh red persimmons in a dish
　　　　　are beautiful indeed.
Though they are not pomeloes,
　　　　　yet I could still pocket them.
But I have no one to make happy with them;
　　　　　so they make me sad.

PAK INNO (1561–1642)

A song of filial piety by a poet whose work is mostly disfigured by musty didacticism. The reference is to Lü Chi of the later Han, who when he was five years old was given some pomeloes but instead of eating them took them home to his mother. This story becomes a stock example of filial piety. The implication of the sijo is that the poet's parents are dead.

THE SONG OF THE FIVE FRIENDS

42

If you ask, how many friends have I:
　　　　　water and rocks, pine and bamboo;
The moon rising on the east hill—
　　　　　that also makes me happy.
Now I ask, beyond these five friends,
　　　　　what need is there for any more?

43

The clouds' color is good they say,
　　　　　but often they grow leaden;
The breezes' voice is clear they say,
　　　　　but too often it is stilled.
And I say that the waters alone
　　　　　are always good and flowing.

44

Why do flowers blossom,
                    and just as quickly fade?
Why does the grass grow green,
                    while it yellows and withers away?
Can it be that only the rocks
                    are quite immune from all this change?

45

On warm days the flowers bloom,
                    on cold days the leaves fall,
Yet, pine, how is it that you
                    are untouched by frost and snow?
I am sure that it must be
                    because your roots reach to the Nine Springs.

46

This one is not a true tree,
                    neither is it a grass.
Who made it grow up so straight?
                    And why is it so clean inside?
I like it for these two qualities,
                    and for being always green.

Tiny object floating on high
          giving light to all the world,
Could any other light
          shine so brightly in the dark night?
What you see you do not tell of.
          Can I say you are my friend?

YUN SŎNDO (1587–1671)

Although Yun Sŏndo's range of imagery is less bold than that of Chŏng
Ch'ŏl, many Koreans regard Yun Sŏndo as the greater poet of the two.
After early success in official life he was banished for imprudent crit-
icism of those in power. Thirteen years later he returned and became
tutor to the royal princes Pongnim and Inp'yŏng (see Nos. 12 and 20).
He spent most of his life in rustic retirement away from court. His most
famous composition is "The Fisherman's Calendar," Nos. 183–222.
    The Nine Springs (*chiu-ch'üan*) in No. 45 means the nether world,
deep at the center of the earth.

SONGS OF THE PLUM BLOSSOM

48

Immature, gaunt branches,
          I did not believe your promise.
But I see you have kept faith
          with a few handfuls of blossom.
When I come with a candle to tend you,
          The faintest fragrance floats on the air.

49

The sun sets. Does the moon rise
                to keep a tryst it's made with you,
Flowers that were hidden in the room,
                but now give fragrance, as in greeting?
A strange thing: the plum blossom and the moon
                are friends, but I never knew.

50

Pure as ice and white as jade,
                there you are amid the snow,
Silently breathing fragrance
                to keep your tryst with the moon at dusk.
Can there be grace and loyalty
                to equal yours, I wonder?

51

You made a promise with the snow,
                and now you have blossomed.
The moon is rising through the dusk
                and the shadows take strange forms.
Fresh fragrance is poured into the cup,
                and I shall enjoy getting drunk.

52

Those flowers hidden in the East Pavilion,
        are they rhododendrons or azaleas?
Earth and sky are full of snow—
        how have they managed to bloom?
Now I see: Spring warmth in the snows—
        what can they be but plum blossoms?

53

The wind has swept the snowdrifts
        up to the windows of the mountain cottage;
Bitter air finds its way in
        and attacks the dormant plum blossom.
However hard you try to freeze them,
        Spring has come and you cannot stop it.

54

Beyond the sea, in the snows of Lo-fu shan,
        on a rough and rugged tall black stump of tree,
With what strange strength have you sent out branches
        and even blossomed thus with flowers?
Though no more than half a rotten stump remains,
        will that not do to herald spring?

55

"Going round the eaves and laughing with the plum blossom,"
> "The subtle fragrance floats in the autumn dusk."

It is already cold enough,
> why should it be snowing too?

Maybe the signs of spring in the bedroom
> make the cold envious?—I wonder.

AN MINYŎNG (19th century)

The eight "Songs of the Plum Blossom" (*Maehwa-sa* or *Yŏngmae-sa*) are said to have been composed by An Minyŏng when he was present at a party with friends and singing girls in the early spring of 1841 at the house of his teacher, Pak Hyogwan. A blossoming branch of plum had been set on the table by Pak, and An performed this small tour-de-force in its honor, using the traditional imagery of plum blossom blooming in the snow as a symbol of loyalty.

An collaborated with Pak in editing the *Kagok wŏllyu*.

Lo-fu shan (No. 54) is a mountain in the Kwang-tung province of China, famous for its flowers.

In the last poem the first line is a direct quotation, in Chinese, from Tu Fu, and the second, again in Chinese, is quoted from the Sung poet Lin Pu.

Songs of Loyalty

56

Though this frame should die and die,
    though I die a hundred times,
My bleached bones all turn to dust,
    my very soul exist or not—
What can change the undivided heart
    that glows with faith toward my lord?

CHŎNG MONGJU (1337–1392)

A popular legend says that during the last days of the Koryŏ dynasty
the son of the rising general Yi toasted the great scholar P'oŭn (Chŏng
Mongju) with a taunting song, suggesting the great scholar join the
general's side. P'oŭn replied with this poem, which has become a
classic example of Korean fidelity—especially in one phrase of the last
line meaning, literally, "one-piece red heart."

This is perhaps the best known of all sijo, made more heroic by the
fact that shortly after composing it Chŏng was assassinated by the Yi
faction at the Sŏnjuk Bridge in Kaesŏng.

When this frame is dead and gone
>>>>what will then become of me?
On the peak of Pongnae-san
>>>>I shall become a spreading pine.
When white snow fills heaven and earth
>>>>I shall still stand lone and green
>>>SŎNG SAMMUN (1418–1456)

Sŏng Sammun was one of the Six Martyred Subjects who attempted to reinstate the deposed boy king Tanjong. He was also one of the scholars who were employed by Sejong in the creation of the Korean alphabet. Pongnae-san is the name poetically applied to the Diamond Mountains in the summertime, and might be freely paraphrased as "Fairyland of Foliage." The song begins with a deliberate quotation from a previous loyalist poem, that of Chŏng Mongju, and contrasts this summer name of the Diamond Mountains with Chŏng's phrase "bleached bones," which is their winter name.

This poem is discussed at length in the Introduction.

A little bunch of parsley,
>>>>which I dug and rinsed myself.
I did it for no one else,
>>>>but simply to give it to you.
The flavor is not so very pungent;
>>>>taste it, once more taste it, and see.
>>>YU HŬICH'UN (1513–1577)

Usually interpreted as an expression of continuing loyalty from a courtier retired to the countryside. The poet spent twenty years of his life as an exile in Cheju, the large island off south Korea.

The parsley is the Korean *minari*.

59

The morning is cold and frosty.
                    Fresh yellow chrysanthemums
Overflow their silver bowl
                    bestowed upon the Jade Hall.
Do not compare them to peach and plum blossom;
                    the King's meaning is clear.

SONG SUN (1493–1583)

The poet was a high-grade civil servant. King Myŏngjong sent the
flowers to the royal archives house or Hongmun-gwan (the Jade Hall)
asking for a poem, but the people there were unable to produce one and
got Song to do it for them. The king was delighted and rewarded the
poet royally.

The chrysanthemum has bloomed in the frost—this adds extra force
to the usual symbolism of the chrysanthemum as the flower of the good
and wise man. Yellow was a royal color. The contrast with peach and
plum blossom is also a contrast with the sensuous pleasures associated
with spring.

Some editions have a golden bowl instead of a silver one, and three
anthologies attribute the poem to Chŏng Ch'ŏl.

60

How comes it, chrysanthemum,
                    when Orient Spring has long since passed—
Leaves fall, heaven freezes—
                    you alone are in full bloom?
Can none but you vanquish the frosts
                    in solitary loyalty?

YI CHŎNGBO (1693–1766)

Orient Spring in Korean is literally "East Wind of the Third Moon,"
and implies the association of the East with the spring season in the
"Five Elements Theory" of Chinese cosmogony.

61

Could my heart but be removed
>> and assume the moon's bright shape
To be hung there bright and shining
>> in the vast expanse of heaven,
I could go where my dear lord is,
>> and pour my light upon him.

CHONG CH'ŎL (1536–1593)

62

Paulownia leaves are falling,
>> so I know that autumn has come.
Fine rain on the clear stream
>> makes the night air fresh and cool.
But my lord is a thousand leagues away
>> and thoughts of him keep me awake.

CHONG CH'ŎL (1536–1593)

63

Snow has fallen on the pine-woods,
>> and every bough has blossomed.
I should like to pluck a branch
>> and send it to where my lord is.
After he has looked at it,
>> what matter if the snow-flowers melt?

CHONG CH'ŎL (1536–1593)

In my breast a blazing fire

        consumes heart, liver, reins, and lungs.

In a dream I saw Shen Nung,

        and asked him for an antidote.

Such fire comes of pride and loyal shame.

        It can't be quenched, he told me.

        PAK T'AEBO (1654–1689)

Shen Nung, the Divine Husbandman, was a legendary emperor of primeval China who is credited with having invented medicine, among other things. The poet is lamenting the decay of the country.

Pak T'aebo was an official who incurred royal displeasure by protesting against the demission of Queen Inmok. He was sent into exile, but died on the way, at Noryang-jin, near Seoul. Subsequently he was reinstated and honored with a posthumous title.

Love Songs

65

I thought about that fan
           and why you sent it to me . . .
You must have meant me
           to puff out the flame in my heart.
But my tears cannot quench it,
           so what use will a fan be?

ANONYMOUS

66

The blue hills are my desire,
           the green streams my loved one's love.
Though the green streams flow on,
           can the blue hills remove?
And the streams, crying as they depart,
           can they forget the blue hills?

HWANG CHINI (early 16th century)

Chini was a clever girl of legendary beauty who is said to have lived in Kaesŏng. A number of well-known stories tell how she could seduce the gravest of scholars.

67

If my tears were made of pearls,
        I would catch them all and save them.
When you came back ten years later,
        a jeweled castle should enthrone you.
But these tears leave no trace at all.
        So I am left desolate.

ANONYMOUS

68

My horse neighs and strains to go
        but you hold me and won't let me leave.
The sun has already passed over the hill,
        and I have a thousand leagues to cover.
Let go, love: don't try to hold me back;
        go and stop the setting sun!

ANONYMOUS

69

I cling to your sleeve;
        heed my tears and do not go.
The sun has already
        sunk beyond the distant hills.
If you trim the flickering guest-room lamp
        and stay awake you'll know my pain.

YI MYŎNGHAN (1595–1645)

The poet was a distinguished scholar-statesman.

This is all my doing!
> Did I not know I loved him so?
If I had bid him stay,
> Would he have gone? But I did it—
I sent him away: and, ah me,
> I did not know he was so dear.

HWANG CHINI (early 16th century)

Some editions attribute this poem to King Sŏngjong (reigned 1470–1494). In that case it is understood to express regret over the dismissal of a minister.

You have been gone such a long time—
> even for a moment, could I forget you?
In the drizzling rain on the spring river,
> mandarin ducks enjoy themselves;
But at night cold tears soak my lonely pillow,
> and how can you know, my beloved?

HO SŎKKYUN (19th century?)

Mandarin ducks are a traditional symbol of conjugal fidelity. Spring is the season for love, and rain is common in poems of yearning for a departed lover.

Nothing is known of the poet. Sixteen sijo are attributed to him in a nineteenth-century anthology.

72

A lover seen in dreams

    will never prove faithful, they say.
But when I yearn and long for you,

    how can I see you, save in dreams?
O Lover, though it be in dreams,

    let me see you, all the time!

MYŎNGOK (late 18th century)

Myŏngok was a *kisaeng*, or professional woman entertainer, of Suwŏn.
Her name means "Bright Jade."

73

"Love." It is a lying word.

    That you love me, another lie.
"The loved one is seen in dreams."

    That is still a greater lie.
How can I, who can never sleep,

    hope to see you in my dreams?

KIM SANGYONG (1561–1637)

The poet was a brother of a prime minister and himself became Minister of Justice. At the time of the Manchu invasions he was unable to defend Kanghwa and so committed suicide by blowing himself up with gunpowder.

74

If on the pathways of dreams
                    a footprint could leave a mark,
The road by your window
                    though rough with rocks,
                    would soon wear smooth.
But in dreams paths take no footprints.
                    I mourn the more for that.

YI MYŎNGHAN (1595–1645)

75

If we could change in the next life,
                    and you become me and I be you,
And you begin to yearn for me
                    as I have always yearned for you,
Then indeed, it would be your turn to suffer
                    and know my pain. How about that?

ANONYMOUS

I chose a wild willow branch
>and plucked it to send it to you.
I want you to plant it
>by the window where you sleep.
When new leaves open in the night rains,
>think it is I that have come to you.

HONGNANG (16th century)

Hongnang was a kisaeng of Kyŏngsŏng, in the furthest northeast part of Korea. She became very fond of Ch'oe Kyŏngch'ang while he was in Kyŏngsŏng on a government duty tour and followed him part of the way back to Seoul. When she parted from him she is said to have fitted this song to the gift of a wild willow branch. Eventually she joined him in Seoul and the liaison led to his public disgrace.

A willow branch was customarily given to a traveler setting out on a journey in pre-T'ang China.

77

I will break in two the long strong back
>of this long midwinter night,
Roll it up and put it away
>under the springtime coverlet.
And the night that my loved one comes back again
>I will unroll it to lengthen the time.

HWANG CHINI (early 16th century)

The word used for "roll up" is a pun on "frosty cold," and the word used for the loved one is a pun on "frozen," hinting that he had turned cold. Springtime is the time for love-making as well as of shortening nights. The poem is one of the best known and most widely quoted of all sijo.

78

O moon, O shining round moon,
        O moon that shines in my beloved's room!
Is he sleeping there alone,
        or does he clasp some other girl?
I beg you to tell me the truth, moon:
        it is life and death to me.

ANONYMOUS

79

Ride a horse through a field of flowers
        and fragrance will spring from his hoofs.
Enter within the Wine Springs Hall
        and scent from untouched wine will stick.
But why when I only looked at him
        does word of my love spread abroad?

ANONYMOUS

Wine Springs (Chiu-ch'üan) is a legendary Chinese name referring to the place where the spring water tasted like wine. It was used by the T'ang poets in drinking songs.

He is late for our tryst;

        the flowers of the green peach have all shattered.

I wonder whether that magpie

        which called this morning was faithful.

No matter; I'll take my mirror

        and touch up my eyebrows afresh.

            ANONYMOUS

The magpie is a symbol of good news, especially if heard in the early morning.

    The green peach has a bitter fruit but a beautiful multi-petaled white flower. Lao-tzŭ in the Western Paradise is said to have eaten a green peach that was sweet together with a purple pear in a collation with the Queen Mother of that region.

The drum sounds in the South Pavilion,

        the Milky Way shines in the Third Watch.

A young man's heart is

        all for whipping a white horse down the road,

But no one waits behind the gauze screen,

        and so I stay standing sadly here.

            ANONYMOUS

The incense has burnt out in the golden censer,
>   the drops of the water clock are running late.
Where have you been?
>   Whose love have you been enjoying?
Already the moon has reached the balustrade:
>   Have you come to feel my pulse?
>   KIM SANGYONG (1561–1637)

This poem is based on one by the Sung poet Wang An-shih.

Beloved, you're smooth as a watermelon,
>   but don't use honeydew words to me.
Your words come thick as aubergines,
>   but they are crooked as gherkins.
Give up your hollow talk,
>   empty as candied gourds in autumn.
>   ANONYMOUS

This poem is discussed in the Introduction.

Clutching a purple coat round her head
>   on a drizzling rainy day,
That girl is running as fast as she can
>   to the village where the pear trees are in bloom.
I wonder whose false promises
>   have made her ignore her soaking clothes?
>   ANONYMOUS

85

Oh, I caught sight of him!
          I caught sight of that handsome monk,
With his slender pretty body
          wrapped up in his faded old robe—
He was like a branch of camellia
          in an old hollow pine in deep snow.

ANONYMOUS

86

Last night I slept alone, curled up like a shrimp;
          and the night before I slept alone,
          curled up like a shrimp.
What sort of life is this? Every night without a break,
          I always sleep alone, curled up like a shrimp.
But today the man I love has come:
          I wonder whether I'll stretch my legs
          and sleep relaxed tonight?

ANONYMOUS

87

The northern sky seemed clear,
          so I set off without a cloak;
But snow has appeared on the mountains
          and cold rain fills the fields.
Today I met with chilly showers:
          shall I freeze in bed tonight?

IM CHE (1549–1587)

Im Che was a famous philanderer and poet, though his stubbornness kept him from high office. Here he puns on the name of Hanu (Chilly Showers), who was a kisaeng of P'yŏngyang. Her reputed reply was also a sijo:

88

What's all this talk of freezing?
          Why should you be cold tonight?
With a duck-broidered pillow and kingfisher quilt,
          how can you freeze tonight?
Today you have met Chilly Showers:
          will you melt in bed, I wonder?

The duck-broidered pillow had on it mandarin ducks, a symbol of conjugal fidelity.

89

Butterfly, come to the blue hills!
          You come too, striped swallowtail!
If we find it's drawing late,
          we'll crawl inside a flower to sleep.
If the flower does not receive us well,
          we'll find a leaf and sleep out there.

ANONYMOUS

This should probably be read as a convivial masculine song. The butterfly and the flower as symbols of the lover and his girl would not have been lost on eighteenth-century sijo singers.

As I passed along the road
>I turned aside at the scent of flowers.
A squash flower! It is a flower,
>but butterflies do not dally there.
Hurry, boy! Turn my shoes around.
>I must strike the road again.

ANONYMOUS

A song from the "Flower and Willow World" of women entertainers and courtesans, where flowers are a traditional symbol of pretty women and butterflies of men. Here the customer was disappointed. The shoes have to be turned around because they are kicked off at the door on entering and must be turned around to be put on when leaving.

(I have not yet found this song in any printed collection. It was recited to me by an old gentleman in a railway train.)

Pretty one, when I seize your wrist,
>do you laugh at me so coyly?
Over your shoulder I stroke your back,
>feeling further till we embrace—
"No sir, stop! Wander no further!
>My breast is beginning to throb."

ANONYMOUS

92

My beloved roars like the thunder,
          and I meet him like sheet lightning;
Like the rain he comes in showers,
          then like the clouds we part again.
In my breast an empty sigh is born like the wind,
          like a sad mist spreading round.

ANONYMOUS

Rain and clouds are a traditional symbol for sexual congress.

93

"What was love like?
          Was it round? Was it wide?
Was it long? Was it short?
          Could you pace it? Could you span it?"
"It was not long enough to tire me,
          but it was enough to sever my entrails."

ANONYMOUS

This is one of the best known of the anonymous love poems. It exists in several versions.

Songs of Solitude

94

I hung green jade chimes by the window,
  with a screen of peacock feathers beneath.
Whenever the wind blows they flutter,
  and beguile me with their tinkling sound.
In the night it penetrates my sleep,
  like the sound of distant temple bells.

ANONYMOUS

95

The wild geese have all flown away,
  already the frosts have come;
The autumn night is dark and long
  and so are travelers' cares.
But moonlight floods the midnight yard,
  and I seem to be at home.

CHO MYŎNGNI (1697– ?)

Like many statesmen of the Yi period, Cho Myŏngni had his time in exile. The imagery of geese, frost, moonlight, and an inn room on an autumn night is found in so many sijo that it has become a cliché for homesickness; but this particular song is raised above the common level by its positive conclusion.

In Lo-yang town I feel the autumn wind,
            I want to write home, ideas crowd my mind.
Anxious that I may have left something out,
            though the messenger is ready,
            I break the seal again.
Possibly someone else will be going
            who can deliver my letter.

ANONYMOUS

Another example of a complete Chinese poem worked into a sijo. The first and middle lines are quoted from *Ch'iu-szŭ* by the T'ang poet Chang Chi.

It rained during the night,
            and pomegranates have all burst into bloom.
I sit in the lotus lake pavilion
            with the curtain of crystal beads rolled up.
As ever, my efforts are vain
            to forget him who makes me sad.

SIN HŬM (1566–1628)

Sin Hŭm was another of the statesmen who suffered under the irrational rule of Kwanghae-gun, but during the following reign he rose to be prime minister.

The middle line alludes to a poem by Li Po about a girl disappointed in love, but the sijo may refer to the king.

98

The raindrops come pattering
        heartlessly on the paulownia.
My sorrow is great
        and the sound in the leaves is sad.
After this would anyone have the heart
        to plant a tree with such broad leaves?

KIM SANGYONG (1561–1637)

99

Paulownias are planted
        to make the phoenixes come.
Is it only when I set one,
        that though I wait, they do not come?
Nothing but the moon, round and bright,
        gets caught up there in the bare branches.

ANONYMOUS

The oriental phoenix, which brings blessings, is said to roost only on the paulownia tree. It is also a symbol of conjugal affection.

The paulownia tree in question is not the true or royal paulownia (*Paulownia tomentosa*) but the parasol tree or phoenix tree (*Firmiana platanifolia*) called the "green paulownia" in Korean because the bark of the trunk and branches remains bright green throughout the tree's life.

No. 225 is a sasŏl treatment of the same theme.

By the stream in the valley
　　　　　I leaned on a rock and made a house;
I ploughed the fields of the moonlight
　　　　　and I lay down on a bed of clouds.
Heaven and earth both spoke to me and said:
　　　　　Let us grow old together here.

ANONYMOUS

Two stone buddhas by the roadside
　　　　　face each other, naked and unfed.
In wind, rain, snow and frosts
　　　　　they sit there unprotected.
Yet they know nothing of mankind's partings:
　　　　　and just for that I envy them.

CHŎNG CH'ŎL (1536–1593)

Songs of Music

102

The Great String of the Black Lute quavers
     and my heart is softly melted.
With martial pizzicato
     the Sage String inspires a strong will.
Here, there is no hint of sadness,
     so how can I think of parting?

CHŎNG CH'ŎL (1536–1593)

The Black Lute is the noblest of Korean instruments. In this and the
following poem Chŏng Ch'ŏl speaks of the peculiar qualities of some
of its many strings. The parting in the last line may refer to reluctance
to lay the lute aside.

103

The Great String of the Black Lute sounds
     as I move the goosefoot along,
Like water that was icebound
     bursting booming into the stream.
Now I hear raindrops falling on lotus leaves:
     are they trying to match this music?

CHŎNG CH'ŎL (1536–1593)

The goosefoot is the tiny bridge or stop that can be moved along under
each string of the lute.

How lovely! like walking in moonlight
>with the breeze in one's silken sleeves!

Lingering before flowers
>fits the feelings of a lover.

Loveliest of all the dances
>is this Dance of the Orioles in Spring!

KING IKCHONG (1809–1830)

Ikchong never reigned as king, but because his son became King Hŏnjong, he was subsequently canonized as Ikchong. This song was composed for a palace banquet in honor of his mother, Queen Sunwan. The Dance of Orioles in Spring, a solo by a single female dancer on a flowered rush mat, was performed at the party.

Songs of Mortality

105

If you weep for your dead husband
                your tears will roll down both your breasts,
Your milk will be salty and then
                your baby will be fractious.
You poor thing! Why should anybody
                have to be born a woman?
          CHŎNG CH'ŎL (1536–1593)

106

Green grass covers the valley.
                Do you sleep? Are you at rest?
O where is that lovely face?
                Can mere bones lie buried here?
I have wine, but no chance to share it.
                Alone, I pour it sadly.
          IM CHE (1549–1587)

This song marks a visit to the grave of the famous kisaeng poetess Hwang Chini (see No. 66).

107

"Peach blossom, explain to me
             why you first don pink cosmetic,
Then, in drizzling rain
             sadly pour so many tears?"
"I am sad because the springtime
             will so quickly pass and go."

ANONYMOUS

108

The East Prince has come again
             and everything rejoices.
Grass and trees and insects
             every year return to life.
Why is it that man alone,
             once he has gone cannot return?

PAK HYOGWAN (late 19th century)

The poet was a favorite of the Taewŏn-gun, who is equally famous for his isolationist policies and his delicate brush drawings of orchids. Pak Hyogwan was also compiler, together with his pupil An Minyŏng, of a famous sijo anthology, *Kagok wŏllyu*. Translations of An's work can be found at Nos. 48–55, and 124.

The East Prince is the springtime.

109

The hills have stood from of old;
> but streams are never ancient waters.
Day and night they flow on:
> how can they ever endure?
Famous men are like the waters:
> they pass and they cannot return.

HWANG CHINI (early 16th century)

The poetess was the famous kisaeng of Kaesŏng.

110

Stay, O wind, and do not blow:
> the leaves of the weeping tree by the arbor
> are all fallen.
Months and years, stay in your course:
> fair brow and fresh face alike grow old.
Think of man: he cannot stay young forever;
> that's what makes me sad for him.

ANONYMOUS

111

Misery! They deceived me!
> Autumn moon and spring breeze,
> they deceived me!
Each season returned in time
> and I believed they were faithful.
But they left me with my greying hair
> and chased away to find more youngsters.

ANONYMOUS

112

My heart, why do you always
　　　　　seem to be growing younger?
When I am growing old,
　　　　　why do you not grow old too?
I wonder, should I follow you,
　　　　　and laugh at other people?

 SŎ KYŎNGDŎK (1489–1546)

113

Do not envy the freedom
　　　　　of the fish that play in the water:
When the fishers have gone
　　　　　the egret soon comes in their place.
All day long, diving up and down,
　　　　　the fish have no rest from fear.

YI CHŎNGBO (1693–1766)

114

Faithful old bamboo stick,
　　　　　I am glad to see you again.
What fun when I was a boy
　　　　　to straddle you and call you a horse!
Come out now from under the window
　　　　　and let me walk behind you.

KIM KWANGUK (1580–1656)

Kim Kwanguk also suffered under the tyrant Kwanghae-gun and was exiled, but was reinstated under the subsequent king. This is the ninth poem in a fourteen-song cycle inspired by the rustic poetry of the pre-T'ang poet T'ao Yüan-ming (also known as T'ao Ch'ien, 372–427). It is entitled *Yulli yugok* ("Reliques of Chestnut Village"), after T'ao's village of the same name, Li-li. No. 161 is taken from the same cycle.

115

My ageing affections
        I'll beguile with chrysanthemums,
My tangled skein of worries
        I'll beguile with ink drawings of grapevines,
The white hair straying under my ears
        I'll beguile with one long song.
           KIM SUJANG (1690– ?)

116

Do we have two or three lives?
        Do we have four or five bodies?
In this span of borrowed life,
        we bear but a body of dreams.
All life long we are busy with living:
        when shall we have time to play?
           ANONYMOUS

117

Fishes in the palace pond,
        did you come by yourselves, or did someone
        catch and bring you?
You left the clear deeps of the North Sea
        and somehow you came here.
Willing or not, you cannot get out:
        your lot is the same as mine.
           ANONYMOUS

The author is thought to have been one of the many palace women, condemned to a barren and boring life unless they were selected as royal concubines.

Songs of Nature

118

A boy comes by my window,
          saying today is the New Year.
I open the eastern lattice—
          the usual sun has risen again.
See here, boy! It's the same old sun.
          Come tell me when a new one dawns!
        CHU ŬISIK (18th century)

119

Two days ago for the first time
          I stroked the last falcon of the brood,
I trimmed bells on its jesses
          and took it out in the evening sun.
In all life shall any man find again
          greater contentment than this?
        KIM CH'ANGŎP (1658–1721)

120
Last night's wind spoiled the blossoms
        of every peach tree in the garden.
Is the boy fetching a broom?
        Does he mean to sweep them up?
Fallen flowers, but still they are flowers:
        what need is there to sweep them?

ANONYMOUS

121
Pear blossoms hither and thither
        toss about madly in the wind,
Unable to settle on branches
        they get caught in spiders' webs.
The spider knows nothing of flowers,
        but thinks it's caught a butterfly.

YI CHŎNGBO (1693–1766)

122
Forty thousand bushels of bright beads
        have fallen on the lotus leaves.
The full leaves seem to measure them,
        but what will they do with them—
Spattering bouncing raindrops,
        exhilarating and joyous?

CHŎNG CH'ŎL (1536–1593)

123

The valleys are all submerged
> in white clouds and bluish mists,
The maples crimsoned by the fall
> are lovelier than the flowers of spring.
Great Heaven has adorned the mountains,
> and has done it all for me.

KIM CH'ŎNT'AEK (18th century)

124

The night wind whirls the snowstorm
> in the empty hills, returning traveler.
The dog barks at the yard gate,
> can you hear him or can't you hear?
The stony path is buried under snow:
> let's get that donkey's harness off.

AN MINYŎNG (19th century)

This is a familiar subject for Korean watercolors, and thus reflects something of the narrowing scope of nineteenth-century Korean composition.

The *Kagok wŏllyu* says that this poem was written when An Minyŏng visited Pak Hyogwan's country cottage on a stormy night.

125

White snow still covers all the earth,
> the mountains glow like pale jade.
Plum blossom is half open,
> bamboo buds are bursting green.
Come my lad, fill the cup to the brim,
> the spring feeling is on us!

ANONYMOUS

126

Pallid moon on pear blossom,
   midnight and the Milky Way—
The crying cuckoo tells my heart
   the news of spring.
This feeling is like a sickness:
   it prevents me from sleeping.

   YI CHONYŎN (1269–1343)

Reputedly a very early poem indeed, from the hand of a Koryŏ states-
man. One interpretation of the poem would have it that the poet was
on an embassy to the Mongol (Yüan) court at Peking and suffering
from homesickness.

However, traditional Korean feeling about the springtime is mel-
ancholy. In contrast to the exuberant gaiety which characterizes the
spring lyrics of medieval Europe, Korean reaction to spring is dom-
inated by thoughts of the lean season before the new crops ripen, the
beginning of the year's hard work, and the incidence of warm-weather
diseases.

127

My horse is startled and shies.
   I tug the rein and stop to look:
The green-embroidered mountains
   are upside down in the water.
Little horse, don't be afraid:
   this is what I came out to see.

   ANONYMOUS

128

Blue mountains gently gently,
  green waters gently gently;
Hills gently gently, streams gently gently,
  and between them I too gently gently—
In the midst, gently gently, this body growing older;
  gently gently shall it be.

SONG SIYŎL (1607–1689)

This poem is sometimes attributed to Kim In-hu (1510–1560) but more often to Song Siyŏl—also known as Uam—one of Korea's greatest writers and a promoter of Neo-Confucianism.

Song Siyŏl was present at the siege of Namhan-sansŏng, the mountain fortress east of Seoul where the king and government took refuge during the Manchu invasion and eventually capitulated. Song was constantly involved in political strife, and finally committed suicide, at the king's command, in Chŏngŭp. He was canonized in Korea as a Confucian sage.

This poem expresses contentment after political downfall.

129

The blue mountains utter no word,
  the waters flow without form,
The clear breeze cannot be bought,
  the shining moon has no owner.
Among these I can live free from sickness,
  I shall grow old without worries.

SŎNG HUN (1535–1598)

Sŏng Hun also suffered political exile during a time of factional struggle. He was a friend of Yulgok and Chŏng Ch'ŏl.

130

I look down through far green depths,

        then look round at piled blue peaks.

Oh, how pitiful

        the world with all its red dust!

And moonlight makes these lakes and streams

        even more unworldly.

        YI HYŎNBO (1467–1555)

"Red dust" is a traditional symbol for the cares of political and urban life.

    Confucius said: The wise delight in water, the virtuous delight in mountains. (*Analects* VI 21).

131

The moon shines bright, the moon shines brightly now;

        I row my boat on the autumn stream.

The sky is down in the water,

        and high in the sky hangs the shining moon.

Come, pretty lad! fish out that sodden moon:

        we must play ball with it!

        PAK SANG (18th century?)

The poet is known by this sijo only. Another version of the final phrase reads: "let us get drunk by its light."

Riding a blue ox sidesaddle,
>I cross the flowing green waters.
I am going to dig the plant of long life
>in the deep valleys of T'ien-t'ai-shan.
But every valley is shrouded in white clouds
>and I do not know the way.

AN CHŎNG (1494– ?)

An was a local governor who was famous for his calligraphy and his brush drawings of plum blossom and bamboo.

The blue ox is the animal on which Lao-Tzŭ rode away to the west. T'ien-t'ai shan is a mountain in the province of Che-kiang in China. It is traditionally regarded as a center of taoism and an abode of the fairies and immortals. It is also often referred to as the place where the elixir plant abounds.

A shadow strikes the water below:
>a monk passes by on the bridge.
"Stay awhile, reverend sir,
>let me ask you where you go."
He just points his staff at the white clouds
>and keeps on his way without turning.

CHŎNG CH'ŎL (1536–1593)

134

That temple with the throbbing drum
        is far away—but far? How far?
Up among the blue hills,
        beneath the white clouds, I know,
But the mists float thick about it.
        Just where it is, I cannot tell.

PAK INNO (1561–1642)

135

"Passing monk, I want to ask you,
        how is the scenery in the East?"
"Only blood-red roses bloom there
        by the ten bright leagues of sand.
White seagulls circle in pairs
        over the distant estuary."

SIN WI (1769–1847)

The red sea-rose (*Rosa rugosa*) of the east coast of Korea is still as famous as the beaches there. The picture of the white sand with the roses and the gulls is taken from a famous long poem about Kangwŏn province by Chŏng Ch'ŏl.

Sin Wi was a prolific writer of verse in Chinese.

Boys digging for lotus roots
　　　　in the shallow waters at sunset,
Take care when you dig the young plants
　　　　that you do not damage the broad leaves,
For fear you will wake the drowsing
　　　　mandarin ducks that nestle under them.

SŎNG SECH'ANG (1481–1548)

The writer was a high government official in a time of fierce party strife. He was several times exiled to the remote countryside.

A poem by Nansŏrhŏn, the famous Korean woman poet (1563–1589), but written in Chinese, deals with the same subject. If the attribution to Sŏng is correct, the sijo must have come first.

Ibises fly mingled in the sunset
　　　　stream and sky are the same color.
I take a small boat and row
　　　　down to the neck of the stream.
An old man in a rain hat on the other side
　　　　asks me to take him with me.

KIM CH'ŎNT'AEK (18th century)

The first line of this poem is based on a poem by the T'ang poet Wang Po.

Rain spatters the lotus pond,
> evening mist wreathes the willows;

The boatman has disappeared,
> leaving his moored boat empty.

In the dusk the seagulls fly back and forth,
> coming and going in pairs.

CHO HŎN (1544–1592)

Cho Hŏn was a statesman whose career suffered violent ups and downs until he levied a troop of volunteers during the Hideyoshi invasions and died in battle at Kŭmsan (not far from Taejon).

THE NINE SONGS OF KOSAN

139

Kosan's Pool of Nine Songs
> is unknown to most people.

I built a reed house there,
> and my friends come to see me.

In this place I muse on Wu-i's beauty
> and can study Master Chu.

140

Where shall we find the first song?
> The sun shines on the Crown Rock,

The mist clears away from the grass,
> the landscape is a picture.

The wine crock is under the pines,
> and I wait for friends to come.

141

Where shall we find the second song?
                    Late spring by the Flowery Rock:
Luxuriant waves of green leaves
                    have borne the flowers away.
This loveliness is hidden from the world.
                    How can I tell of it?

142

Where shall we find the third song?
                    Leaves cover the Emerald Screen.
The birds are alighting
                    and singing in the foliage.
Light breezes brush the flattened pines
                    and summer's sunshine is gone.

143

Where shall we find the fourth song?
                    The sun sets over the Pine Bank.
The rocks are reflected perfectly
                    in the waters of the pool.
Tree and springs make irrepressible joy
                    rise up within my heart.

144

Where shall we sing the fifth song?
        The Secret Arbor is good.
Cool and delightful
        is my study by the water.
Here I can work to my heart's content
        and make poems of moon and breeze.

145

Where shall we find the sixth song?
        Fisher's Gorge has broad waters.
There I and the fish
        and all who come can find delight.
At evening I shoulder my rod
        and walk homeward by moonlight.

146

Where to sing the seventh song?
        Autumn is best at Maple Rock.
Lightly the delicate frost
        embroiders the hanging rocks.
Alone I sit on the cold stone,
        and I forget to go home.

147

Where shall we hear the eighth song?

    The moon shines on the Tinkling Brook.

There I will play on a lute

    with jade pegs and a golden bridge.

Nobody knows the old time songs

    so I enjoy them all alone.

148

Where shall we find the ninth song?

    Winter has come to Munsan;

The fantastic rocks

    are buried under the snow.

Nobody comes here for pleasure now.

    They think there is nothing to see.

YI I (YULGOK) (1536–1584)

Second only to Yi Hwang in the history of Korean thought, Yi I had a distinguished career in government and retired to Kosan in Hwanghae province in 1569. He was an enthusiastic adherent of the doctrines of Chu Hsi, the twelfth-century Chinese confucian thinker, whose ideas became standard in later Korean orthodoxy. His famous pen name, Yulgok, means Valley of Chestnuts.

The seasonal range of the Kosan Songs is interesting. Spring is hardly noticed and autumn gets the chief attention. Autumn is still the reading season in Korea.

The idea of writing Nine Songs is apparently an imitation of the Nine Songs which Chu Hsi wrote about his place of retreat at Wu-i in Fukien province. Yulgok treats Kosan in imagination as Wu-i.

Songs of Retirement and Rustic Life

149

Only I and the seagulls know
> Ch'ŏngnyang-san's thirty-six peaks.
The seagulls are chatterers,
> but falling flowers tell the most tales.
Peach petals, do not float down!
> The fishers will know where we are.

YI HWANG (1501–1570)

Yi Hwang, also known as T'oegye (Ebbing Brook), is Korea's greatest and most original philosopher. He held office at court, but several times retired voluntarily to the countryside where he both studied and taught.

Ch'ŏngnyang-san is in North Kyŏngsang province near Andong. There are other mountain groups in the Orient with the same name. The name means "pure and cool," and is connected with the bliss of Nirvana by Buddhists. It is also the name of a village outside Seoul, now a part of the suburbs.

I doze and wake, take my fishing rod,

> dance a little and forget my rain-cape.

Do not laugh, white seagulls,

> at the antics of an old man.

Ten *li* on, the peaches are in bloom,

> and the spring fever is on me.

ANONYMOUS

A number of favorite sijo themes are here combined—fishing, old age, seagulls, rain, peach blossoms, and spring, but the combination is unique. Cf. No. 190.

151

This morning we'll go fishing,

> tomorrow we'll go hunting,

The next day have a picnic,

> the day after, set up a club.

The fifth day we'll have archery,

> and each bring his own bottle.

KIM YUGI (late 17th century)

The poem is expressive of court nostalgia for the simple camaraderie of country life. The club mentioned is the Korean *kye,* a kind of mutual benefit association, which is often formed purely for the sake of convivial gatherings.

Some versions give a different Chinese reading for the Korean syllables here translated "set up a club" which make them mean "offer a sacrifice," but this accords less well with the rest of the song.

The picnic mentioned is specifically a picnic at which cakes flavored with fresh azalea flowers are made and eaten.

152

Milky rain-mist on the green hills,
        surely you won't deceive me?
Rain-cape of sedge and horsehair hat,
        surely you too won't deceive me?
Two days ago I put off my silken clothes.
        Now I've nothing that can be stained.

CHŎNG CH'ŎL (1536–1593)

The rain-cape of sedge and the horsehair hat are the dress of a farmer.

153

So be my roofbeams short or long,
        my pillars slanting or crooked.
Do not mock my hut
        because it is so tiny.
For the moon and the mountain vines,
        do they not all belong to me?

SIN HŬM (1566–1628)

154

At the end of ten years' work
        I have a hut with a straw roof.
The clear wind lives in one half,
        and the bright moon in the other.
There's no space to invite the hills—
        they will have to stay outside.

SONG SUN (1493–1583)

155

Scarlet-wattled mountain pheasant,
                    falcon perching on the branches,
White egrets searching for fish
                    in the paddy before my house—
should you ever desert my homestead,
                    it will be hard to pass my days.

ANONYMOUS

156

Does dawn light the east window?
                    Already larks sing in the sky.
Where is the boy that tends the ox—
                    has he not yet roused himself?
When will he get his ploughing done
                    in the long field over the hill?

NAM KUMAN (1629–1711)

Nam Kuman was prime minister of Korea. This poem is an example of
deliberate rusticity in a court poet.

157

A boy rides a cow
                    through the willows on the bank;
A rain-drenched traveler
                    asks where he can buy some wine:
"Over there, where the apricot flowers,
                    go there, sir, and ask again."

ANONYMOUS

158

Day has broken once again.
      Let's take our hoes and get out to the fields.
If I get my fields all done,
      then I'll go and help with yours.
Coming home we can gather mulberry leaves
      for the silkworms.

CHŎNG CH'ŎL (1536–1593)

One of a series of didactic poems by a great sixteenth-century poet,
this time encouraging agricultural diligence and cooperation.

159

The day-star's set, the larks are in the sky.
      Shouldering a hoe I leave my yard.
There is heavy dew in the woods,
      my hempen shorts are soon soaked.
Come now, lad, when times are good,
      does it matter if your clothes get wet?

YI CHAE (1725–1776)

160

I will sluice water into the rice field
      and weed the cotton patch,
Then cut cucumbers under the hedge
      and boil the barley for lunch.
If the wine is ready next door,
      get some—even if it means credit.

YI CHŎNGBO (1693–1766)

Scour the earthenware cauldron,

   draw spring water from under the rock,

Seethe some sweet bean porridge,

   set out some brine-pickled herbs—

These two tastes are the best in the world.

   I wonder how many know it.

   KIM KWANGUK (1580–1656)

This is the fourth of a cycle of poems called *Yulli yugok* ("Reliques of Chestnut Village"). No. 114 is from the same cycle.

 Confucius said: With coarse food to eat, water to drink, and my bent arm for a pillow—I still have joy in the midst of these things. (*Analects* VII 15).

You need not spread that straw mat:

   can I not sit on fallen leaves?

Nor light that pinewood torch:

   the moon is up that sank last night.

Don't argue, boy, the wine may be sour,

   and served with weeds, but pour it.

   HAN HO (1543–1605)

Han Ho was a country magistrate, and a famous calligrapher, praised even in China. His pen name was Sŏkpong (Stone Peak).

One cricket cries, "Pe-e-pper ..."
    and another cries, "Sour-sour-sour ..."
Do they mean wild roots are hot,
    homemade wine is rough and raw?
Such as we, buried in the countryside,
    cannot tell what's sour, what's hot ...
        YI CHŎNGJIN (18th century)

This poem depends on two puns. Two kinds of cicada are named in Korean onomatopoetically after their cries, *maemi* and *ssŭrŭrami*. The first puns on the word for peppery taste, and the second the word for sourness. The poem is one more example of the many of the period which lauded the simple life of the rustic.

Are the chestnuts falling fast
    in the vale of russet jujubes,
The crabs already
    crawling in the golden stubble?
Now's the time to get a sieve to strain new wine:
    we must drink with these good things.
        HWANG HŬI (1363–1452)

A reputedly early example of a country poem of the sort that became very popular later on. It is an autumn song, and the chestnuts, Chinese dates, and crabs provide titbits for Korean drinking parties. It reflects the prosperity of the early Yi period, "the reign of great peace."

165

Snow covers the mountain village
    and buries the stony road.
Do not open the brushwood gate,
    for who will come to see me now?
But at night the moon shines brightly:
    shall I say it is my friend?

SIN HŬM (1566–1628)

A gate made of twigs or brushwood is typical of the yard fence of the poorer houses of the countryside.

166

Night covers the mountain village;
    a dog barks in the distance.
I open the brushwood gate
    and see only the moon in a cold sky.
That dog! What is he doing, barking
    at the sleeping moon in the silent hills?

CH'ŎN KŬM

This poem is modeled on the preceding one, though it is not clear to what extent deliberate parody and irony may have been intended. Ch'ŏn Kŭm was a kisaeng who is otherwise unknown.

FOUR SONGS CALLING A BOY

The "boy" of these songs is not necessarily a child, but may be any unmarried man younger than the speaker. The term is more colorless than the English words "boy" or "lad," especially when it is used as the "twist" feature at the beginning of the last line of a sijo, where it has little more force than an interjection. (Cf. Nos. 25, 90, 125.)

167

I. ROOTING ON THE WEST MOUNTAIN

Come my boy, gather up your baskets.
                    Day dies on the western hills.
New born ferns will wither
                    away overnight, will they not?
And what if there were no green ferns,
                    what should I eat at morn and night?

168

II. FISHING IN THE EAST BROOK

Come my boy, bring my straw cloak and hat.
                    The east brook is swollen full.
On my long fishing rod,
                    we'll fix a hook without a barb.
Fishes there! Don't be alarmed.
                    I am only out for sport.

III. PLOUGHING IN THE SOUTH FIELD

Come my boy, get the porridge up.

Much work waits in the south field.

I wonder with whom

I shall share my clumsy plough?

Yet you know, our peaceful ploughing

depends on the king's grace.

IV. DRINKING IN THE NORTH VILLAGE

Come my boy, get the cow ready.

Let's go north and drink new wine.

With rosy countenance

I'll ride home in the moonlight.

Hey nonny! The likes of old King Fu

will ride again tonight.

CHO CHONSŎNG (1553–1627)

Cho lived through the troubled times of internal factions and the Japanese invasion of 1592. He died of sickness during the Manchu invasion of 1627.

The north is symbolic of debauchery, and also of winter. King Fu means the legendary Chinese emperor Fu-hsi, the putative founder of Chinese civilization.

THE TWELVE SONGS OF TOSAN

I. HE SPEAKS OF HIS DESIRES

171

1. What matter if I grow like this,
          what matter if I grow like that?
   What matter if I'm called
          a rustic bore?
   What on earth can cure this craving
          for rocks and flowing springs?

172

2. Let my house be morning mists,
          and my friends the wind and moon;
   While the land is at peace
          I'll decline into old age.
   Just one thing I ask of life:
          that my faults may disappear.

173

3. If they say that grace is gone,
          then they surely speak a lie.
   If they say that man is noble,
          then they surely tell the truth.
   Could it be that all the sages
          have been so much deceived?

4. The orchids in the valley
>> breathe a fragrance in the air,
The white clouds on the mountains
>> offer wonder to the eyes—
In a place like this it is impossible
>> to forget the king's virtues.

5. The terrace fronts the mountain,
>> the water flows below:
Thick flocks of snowy gulls
>> wheel to and fro in the air.
Why, oh why, satin white colt,
>> is your heart set far away?

The white colt is a reference to the Chinese *Book of Songs* and means the mount of an honored guest, here taken as sharing his master's anxiety to leave.

6. Springtime flowers fill the mountains,
>> the autumn moon floods the terrace,
The joys of the year are
>> the stuff of life itself.
Moreover: fish leap, kites soar, clouds pass,
>> and the sun shines:
>> Shall they never have an end?

177

1. Back at the High Cloud Terrace
   my study is cool and quiet.
   A lifetime of books
   has meant delights without end.
   What words can I find to describe
   these pleasures ever fresh?

178

2. The thunder can split the mountain,
   the deaf man will still not hear;
   The noon sun can burn white in mid-heaven,
   the blind man will still not see.
   Men like us, keen-eared, clear-eyed healthy males,
   should not be like the deaf and blind.

179

3. The sages never saw me,
   I never saw the sages.
   I cannot see the sages,
   but their paths still stretch ahead.
   If their paths still stretch ahead,
   then can I not tread them too?

4. Many years have slipped by since
>> I left the path I used to tread.
For awhile I went elsewhere,
>> but at last I have returned.
And now that I have come back,
>> my heart shall never roam again.

5. The green hills—how can it be
>> that they are green eternally?
Flowing streams—how can it be;
>> night and day do they never stand still?
We also, we can never stop,
>> we shall grow green eternally.

6. Even fools can know and can do.
   Is it not easy then?
   Yet even sages cannot know all.
   Is it* not difficult then?
   Pondering whether it's easy or hard
   makes me forget I grow old.

YI HWANG (T'OEGYE) (1501–1570)

These twelve songs were written in 1565, when T'oegye was sixty-four years old. He died in 1570, having spent several periods of life in government service and high office, but always yearning to withdraw to a life of study with a group of disciples. His final retreat was in the beautiful valley of Tosan, in southeast Korea, where his house still stands. T'oegye is unquestionably the greatest of Korean philosophers, one of the few whose theories reached beyond his own country, and these poems with their sometimes heavily Chinese diction, impregnated with his reverence for Chinese philosophy, are a lyrical condensation of his mature doctrine. (See also No. 149.)

THE FISHERMAN'S CALENDAR

Many Korean critics regard this cycle of poems as the highest peak of classical sijo composition. The theme is one that has had wide appeal in the Far East, both literarily and philosophically. It is expressed time and again in the sets of four paintings, one for each season of the year, that are one of the commonest genres of oriental water colors, and significantly the poet refers to this correspondence with painting in the course of his poem. Here each season is represented by a group of ten sijo stanzas.

There were earlier sijo on this subject, some in the form of short cycles, and many single poems, but Yun's is the most extended and unified treatment ever attempted by a Korean poet for any subject. As such it is of unusual importance and interest apart from its intrinsic excellence as poetry.

* "It" is not defined, but all commentators assume it to be the Confucian "way."

The forms of the poems are slightly eccentric. They are most obviously different from all other sijo in the inclusion of two refrains in each stanza. The first refrain differs from stanza to stanza, and tells of the work in the boat in the order in which it is done on a fishing expedition. The same pattern of refrains is used in each of the four sections, imposing a consistent pattern on each quarter of the whole work.

The second refrain, inserted between the second and third lines of the sijo, is purely onomatopoeic. Most other translators have omitted it. However, this rough interruption was intended by the poet, and adds so much to the air of the whole work that it has been retained here. There is a difference of opinion among Korean scholars as to whether *chigukch'ong* represents the sound of the oars or of the anchor chain. The rhythm of the word repeated seems more nearly to suggest the act of rowing. *Ŏshwa* is the only word in these translations which has not been transliterated according to the McCune-Reischauer system. Systematically it should have been written *ŏsăwa*; but to the average reader this is likely to be misleading, because the middle syllable is very lightly pronounced, and a softening of the *s* is normal in modern pronunciation of the equivalent word. It is used to accompany rhythmical physical activity, as for instance by children running together in step (instead of calling "Left, right! Left, right!"). It is the chant of the rower encouraging himself.

The other formal peculiarity of these poems is the syllable count of the verses themselves, as distinct from the refrains. Whereas the typical form of the verse has four phrases to each line, in these poems a line is frequently one phrase short, or else two phrases are compressed into one. Only once does this happen in a first line, but it happens five times in the middle line and nine times in the last line. The last stanza has a very long middle line which is *sui generis*.

The last line also rarely has the heavy second phrase which is so characteristic of most other sijo. The normally strict rule of always beginning the last line with a three-syllable phrase has also been ignored. This phrase (normally the "twist" phrase) can in "The Fisherman's Calendar" have anything from two to five syllables.

There is a corresponding freedom in the application of the

sense structure described in the introduction to this collection. Many of the poems have a triple sense structure without any clear use of a pivot thought or twist. Sometimes the first and middle lines are developed by the last line; sometimes the first two form one developed idea and the last line resolves them.

Perhaps in nothing so much as his confidence in adapting the form did Yun show how skilled he was in meeting the demands of sustained composition; but in the effortless simplicity and spontaneity of his vocabulary and the economy of his images there is equal assurance of a master's art. The material is so simple and commonplace that in the hands of the crowd it is a cliché, but in the hands of the gifted artist it becomes a vehicle for beauty and depth of thought.

I. SPRING

183

1. Mist rises on the stream ahead,
    the sun is on the hill behind.
        Push the boat off, push the boat off!
The night tide has almost gone,
    the morning tide is on its way.
        Chigukch'ong, chigukch'ong, ŏshwa!
Flowers in the distance
    color the river hamlets.

2. The day is warming:
      the fish rise in the water.
            Hoist the anchor! Hoist the anchor!
  Two or three seagulls flying,
      rising and swooping, hover around.
            Chigukch'ong, chigukch'ong, ŏshwa!
  The rods are all ready;
      has the wine flask been put in?

3. An east wind springs up briefly
      and chases pretty ripples.
            Raise the sail, raise the sail!
  We'll go to the Eastern Bay,
      and get there by the Western.
            Chigukch'ong, chigukch'ong, ŏshwa!
  The front mountain passes by us,
      the back mountain comes into view.

4. Is that sound the cuckoo's call?
      is that green the willow grove?
            Row away, row away!
  Two or three fishers' houses
      can be seen through the mist.
            Chigukch'ong, chigukch'ong, ŏshwa!
  Where the stream is deep and clear,
      all kinds of fish are rising now.

5. Basking in the gracious sunshine
   the ripples are as smooth as oil.
   Row away, row away!
   Ought we to cast a net?
   or should we try out a rod?
   Chigukch'ong, chigukch'ong, ŏshwa!
   I feel so much like singing,
   I almost forget the fish.

6. Evening light is slanting low.
   We should stop, and go back home.
   Take down the sail, take down the sail!
   The willows and flowers on the banks
   look different now.
   Chigukch'ong, chigukch'ong, ŏshwa!
   Would this not make statesmen envious?
   Why should I think of their troubles?

7. Let us tread the scented grass,
   and gather tree-root mushrooms.
   Pull the boat in, pull the boat in!
   What did we carry
   with us in this slip of a boat?
   Chigukch'ong, chigukch'ong, ŏshwa!
   When we went, myself alone;
   returning, the moon as well.

8. I have drunk and now I doze;
> the boat takes itself down the stream.
>> *Fasten the boat, fasten the boat!*
> Pink petals are floating about us now;
>> peach orchards must be quite near.
>>> *Chigukch'ong, chigukch'ong, ŏshwa!*
> I am completely
>> removed from the world and its dust.

The peach orchard is a symbol of paradise derived from a prose fragment, *T'ao-hua-yüan-chi* ("The Peach Blossom Spring") by the fourth-century Chinese dilettante T'ao Yüan-ming.

9. Let's pull in the fishing rod,
> See the moon through the awning.
>> *Drop the anchor, drop the anchor!*
> Is it night already?
>> The call of the cuckoo sounds clear.
>>> *Chigukch'ong, chigukch'ong, ŏshwa!*
> I am so endlessly happy,
>> I forget where I should go.

10. Will there not be tomorrow?
    The spring night does not last long.
        Tie the boat fast, tie the boat fast!
    Fishing rods make walking sticks
        as we go to the brushwood gate.
            Chigukch'ong, chigukch'ong, ŏshwa!
    A fisherman's life
        is all passed in this manner.

II. SUMMER

193

1. The long rains have stopped awhile,
    the stream begins to clear itself.
        Push the boat off, push the boat off!
    Shouldering my fishing rod,
        I am beside myself with joy.
            Chigukch'ong, chigukch'ong, ŏshwa!
    Who could it have been
        that made mists, streams, piled peaks?

194

2. Wrap the rice in lotus leaves,
    and don't ask for relishes.
        Hoist the anchor, hoist the anchor!
    I've got my bamboo hat on,
        have you brought my sedge rain-cloak?
            Chigukch'ong, chigukch'ong, ŏshwa!
    That aimless white gull there,
        does he follow me, or I him?

3. The breezes stir in the duckweed,

    the awning is pleasantly cool.

        Raise the sail, raise the sail!

Can you rely on summer winds?

    Let the boat go whither it will.

        Chigukch'ong, chigukch'ong, ŏshwa!

North Bay or South Stream,

    anywhere will do just as well.

4. If the water is muddy,

    then why not wash our feet?

        Row away, row away!

I would go to Wu River

    sadly raging for a thousand years.

        Chigukch'ong, chigukch'ong, ŏshwa!

I would go to Ch'u River,

    but we might land fish with men's souls.

There are three classic Chinese allusions here. A reference to the ancient Songs of Ch'u speaks of washing the hat strings when the water is clear and the feet when the water is muddy, and becomes proverbial for taking life as it comes. The second refers to the anger of Fu Ch'ai of Wu at the suicide of his subject Wu Yüan. He had the body exhumed and thrown into the Wu River in a sack. The third is to an idea that the souls of drowned men pass into fishes, with special reference to Ch'u Yüan of Ch'u.

5. The green willows give thick shade.
      That mossy rock is fantastic.
            Row away, row away!
   When we get down to the bridge,
         avoid the fishermen's squabbles.
            Chigukch'ong, chigukch'ong, ŏshwa!
   If we meet a white-headed old man,
         let's do as they did at Lei Lake.

Legend says that when the Emperor Shun (whose reign Confucius re-
garded as ideal) went to Lei Lake, the people there ceded him the best
place for angling, thus bequeathing an example of good manners. The
fisherman's squabbles would be about rights to good fishing spots.

6. I am so madly happy,
         I scarcely know the long day's done.
            Take down the sail, take down the sail!
   Beating time on the sailmast
         let us sing watermen's songs.
            Chigukch'ong, chigukch'ong, ŏshwa!
   Who can tell how old is this happiness
         of singing as we row?

7. The evening sun is lovely,

    but twilight is closing in.

    Pull the boat in, pull the boat in!

The twisting paths wind through the rocks,

    and bend round under the pines.

    Chigukch'ong, chigukch'ong, ŏshwa!

Among the green leaves on all sides:

    the sound of orioles!

8. Spread the nets out over the sand,

    and let's rest under the awning.

    Fasten the boat, fasten the boat!

Do only mosquitoes bite?

    are the flies not just as bad?

    Chigukch'ong, chigukch'ong, ŏshwa!

And still I have one worry left:

    traitors may eavesdrop here too.

The last phrase refers explicitly to a famous traitor of Han, Sang Hung-yang. Proverbially the flies stand for troublesome people. The sense is that mere mosquitoes are nothing to put up with.

9. Who can tell? Winds and waves
        may suddenly rise in the night.
                Drop the anchor, drop the anchor!
   Who was it that spoke
        of crossing fields in a boat?
                Chigukch'ong, chigukch'ong, ŏshwa!
   Poor humble grasses on the bank:
        I hate to see them crushed.

The middle and last lines quote from a quatrain about a ferryboat by
the T'ang poet Wei Ying-wu.

10. I look for my snail-shell hut,
        it is hidden in white clouds.
                Tie the boat fast, tie the boat fast!
   Exchange my rod for a bullrush fan
        as we start to climb the rock-path.
                Chigukch'ong, chigukch'ong, ŏshwa!
   Did you think I lived idly?
        This is a fisherman's life.

203

1. Away from worldly worries,
   a fisherman's life is the best.
   Push the boat off, push the boat off!
   Do not laugh at old fishers:
   they are painted in every scene.
   Chigukch'ong, chigukch'ong, ŏshwa!
   The four seasons are one pleasure,
   but autumn is best of all.

204

2. When autumn comes to the waterside,
   the fish are all grown fat and sleek.
   Hoist the anchor, hoist the anchor!
   We can ride and glide as we will
   on the clear swell.
   Chigukch'ong, chigukch'ong, ŏshwa!
   Here's what I think of the world of men:
   the further away, the better.

205

3. The white clouds are lifting
   and twigs are rustling in the breeze.
   Raise the sail, raise the sail!
   At high tide we'll go west,
   at low tide we'll move eastward.
   Chigukch'ong, chigukch'ong, ŏshwa!
   White duckweed and pink waterweed
   make every inlet gay.

4. Beyond where the wild geese fly,
  I see mountains I never saw before.
      Row away, row away!
  I have enjoyed all my fishing,
    but here I get the truest joy:
        Chigukch'ong, chigukch'ong, ŏshwa!
  Evening sun is shining
    on a thousand embroidered hills.

5. Jade and silver scales—
    how many fish have I caught?
      Row away, row away!
  Make a fire of reed-stems,
    choose some fish, then broil them.
        Chigukch'ong, chigukch'ong, ŏshwa!
  Turn that earthenware jar upside down
    and fill the gourd with wine.

6. The wind from the side blows gently,
    we come home with sail unfurled.
        Take down the sail, take down the sail!
  The darkness is descending,
    but happiness does not dissolve.
        Chigukch'ong, chigukch'ong, ŏshwa!
  Red trees and clear streams
    are too lovely to grow tired of.

7. A white dew begins to form,

the shining moon is rising now.

Pull the boat in, pull the boat in!

The Phoenix Tower is far away:

to whom can I give this pale light?

Chigukch'ong, chigukch'ong, ŏshwa!

The Jade Hare pounds his simples:

I want to offer them to a great guest.

The Phoenix Tower is the Royal Palace. This is because the phoenix (Chinese *feng*) has been the emblem of virtuous rulers since very early times and a pair of the birds were pictured above the royal throne of Korea. Today the figure is in the standard of the President of Korea. There is a legend about a hare that mixes medicines in a mortar on the moon.

8. Is heaven distinct from the earth?

Then where can this place be?

Fasten the boat, fasten the boat!

West winds cannot cleanse the dust,

what sense is there plying a fan?

Chigukch'ong, chigukch'ong, ŏshwa!

Since I have had nothing to hear,

why should I wash out my ears?

The recluse Hsu Yü was shocked to hear a suggestion that he become king, and went to wash out his ears in a river. Another recluse, Ch'ao-fu, thereafter refused to let his cow drink from that river. The reference is political: Yun is retired from government life and service.

9. Frost congeals on my clothes,
  and yet I do not feel the cold.
      Take down the sail, take down the sail!
  An angler's boat is narrow,
    but the world at large is narrower.
        Chigukch'ong, chigukch'ong, ŏshwa!
  Tomorrow I'll work like this,
    and again the day after that.

10. Go to the stone hut in the pines
    and let's watch the moon at dawn.
        Tie the boat fast, tie the boat fast!
  How can we find the right path
    under fallen leaves in silent hills?
        Chigukch'ong, chigukch'ong, ŏshwa!
  A white cloud follows behind.
    These hermit robes grow heavy.

IV. WINTER

1. When the clouds have passed away,
    the sunshine is bright and warm.
        Push out the boat, push out the boat!
  Heaven and earth are frozen hard,
    and the lake looks ageless.
        Chigukch'ong, chigukch'ong, ŏshwa!
  The boundless, boundless expanse of waves
    is stretched like shimmering silk.

2. Are rod and line ready?
> Have the boat seams all been caulked?
>> *Hoist the anchor, hoist the anchor!*
> They say the nets on the Hsiao and Hsiang,
>> even on Tung-t'ing, freeze.
>>> *Chigukch'ong, chigukch'ong, ŏshwa!*
> At this time there is nowhere
>> better than here for fishing.

The Chinese references are to two famous rivers and the Lake of Tung-t'ing.

3. The fish have left the shallows
> and gone off to deeper waters.
>> *Raise the sail, raise the sail!*
> Now the sun shines a little,
>> let's go and try fishing there.
>>> *Chigukch'ong, chigukch'ong, ŏshwa!*
> They say if the bait is tasty
>> the bigger fish will bite now.

4. After the snow fell last night
      the landscape changed completely.
          Row away, row away!
Ahead are broad glassy acres,
      and behind the jade hills are piled.
          Chigukch'ong, chigukch'ong, ŏshwa!
Fairyland? Buddha-land?
      This place is no world of men.

Fairyland refers here to the paradise of taoism.

5. I have laid by both rod and net,
      drumming the side of the boat,
          Row away, row away!
I wait to cross the stream ahead;
      how many times have I tried it?
          Chigukch'ong, chigukch'ong, ŏshwa!
If only a sudden gust
      would rise and carry me over!

6. How many crows have just flown
    overhead going to roost?
        Take down the sail, take down the sail!
The road in front is growing dark,
    the evening snow falls thickly.
        Chigukch'ong, chigukch'ong, ŏshwa!
Who will attack O-ya Lake
    and conquer the fear of the trees?

O-ya Lake was a place where Li Su of T'ang camouflaged the move-
ments of his troops by freeing flocks of ducks and geese on a snowy
night. The noise of the birds covered the sound of the troops, and the
rebel fortress was conquered. The name was used in Korean form
(Anap Lake) for a royal pond of Silla, still to be seen near Kyŏngju.

"The fear of the trees" refers to the nervousness of the retreating
armies of Chin in 383, who thought every tree held an ambush.

There is probably a reference here also either to Yun Sŏndo's po-
litical enemies (though this is out of tune with the main drift of the
poem) or to Korea's shameful submission to the Manchu dynasty.

7. Rusty cliffs and mossy rocks
    surround us like a painted screen.
        Fasten the boat, fasten the boat!
Big-mouthed, fine-scaled fish—
    have I caught any or not?
        Chigukch'ong, chigukch'ong, ŏshwa!
Alone in my boat I am gay
    with straw cape and reed hat.

8. A lone pine by the water—
> how can it stand there so boldly?
>> *Fasten the boat, fasten the boat!*
> Do not regret those gathering clouds:
>> they will hide the world from us.
>>> *Chigukch'ong, chigukch'ong, ŏshwa!*
> Do not shun the roaring waves:
>> they keep out the noise of crowds.

9. Long ago they said
> that I live in a blessed place.
>> *Drop the anchor, drop the anchor!*
> Who was it that wore sheepskin clothes
> and lived by Ch'i-li River?
>> *Chigukch'ong, chigukch'ong, ŏshwa!*
> What should we think of ten long years,
>> spent fishing with frozen hands?

The man who retired to Ch'i-li River and lived there in sheepskins was Yen Tzü-lung, avoiding the court life of the Han Emperor Kuang-wu. The ten years of cold fishing were done by Chiang T'ai-kung, who went into exile from the Shang tyrant, and was then met and brought back by King Wen of Chou.

10. At last the day has ended,
         it is time to eat and sleep.
              Tie the boat fast, tie the boat fast!
Where red soil in patches shows through
         the wind-strewn snow
        we go singing up the path.
              Chigukch'ong, chigukch'ong, ŏshwa!
Till the moon lights the snow on West Peak
        let's lean on the sill by the pine.

          YUN SŎNDO (1587–1671)

Sasŏl Sijo

From the eighteenth century onwards an expanded form of the sijo called sasŏl sijo came into vogue. It retains the basic threefold structure of the standard form and is composed of similar short phrases of two to five syllables each. Like the standard form, it is intended to be sung. Sometimes one of the three sections has the regular sijo pattern, sometimes only one line is expanded, sometimes only the final brief phrase bears the original sijo stamp. When only one of the lines is expanded the form is distinguished as ŏs-sijo, and has a special musical treatment. Ŏs-sijo means "slightly altered sijo," and sasŏl sijo means "chatty" or "narrative" sijo.

Sasŏl sijo appeared at the time when popular romances began to flourish, and a new pragmatism made itself felt in Korean literature. During this period the life of the common people first became a subject for literature. Most surviving examples are of unknown authorship, and the form is not used by modern poets.

223

The wedding candles flicker in the bedroom
  when I meet this gentle lovely girl.
  I look here, I look there, I look once and again:
  She is fifteen years old,
  and her face is a peach flower.
Golden hairpin and white gauze skirt,
  shining eyes cast sideways,
  and lips half-parted in a smile—
  this is my loved one!
Give me a song to murmur
  and gentleness under the quilt,
  and what more have I to say?
    ANONYMOUS

Like the desperation of a hen pheasant
                chased by a hawk on a mountainside
                without bush or boulder to hide herself.
Like the fear of a sailor in a boat on the high sea,
                loaded with a thousand bags of grain,
                but with the oars lost,
                the sail adrift,
                the rigging frayed,
                the mast broken and the rudder gone,
                the wind howling, the waves billowing,
                wandering in the mist with day swiftly dying
                and a thousand leagues yet left to go,
                darkness on all sides,
                and the water a magpie of blackness and foam,
                when suddenly overtaken by pirates—
Can I say I felt like that
                when I parted from him two days ago?
                ANONYMOUS

A shadow passed on the green gauze screen!
  Thinking only of him, I ran outside to see.
But he did not come.

  The garden was filled with moonlight;
  among the dewy leaves of the parasol tree
  a phoenix had come to rest,
  a shadow bending its neck to preen its feathers.
How lucky that it was nighttime!
  Had it been day,
  I should have been a laughing-stock.
  ANONYMOUS

The parasol tree is the paulownia tree described in No. 99. This is a sasŏl treatment of the same theme, with the less elevated tone that is typical of the sasŏl genre.

226

That blackish, greyish rock over there
  I will attack and chip with a chisel;
I will fashion hair and a pair of horns,
  and turn all the points of a black cow on it.
  o-o-u, o-o-u, o-o-o-o! and keep it.
Then when you come to say goodbye and leave me,
  I'll set you on it backwards and send you away.
  ANONYMOUS

A deliberate satire on a more ecstatic type of love sijo.

227

Ramie thread spun this way and that,
   rolled and wound away on reels.
On the way it is snapped in the middle,
    then sucked and moistened
    by white teeth and red lips,
    then rolled and joined and rubbed
    by the white tips of soft fingers,
    that ramie thread.
Perhaps when my love's love snaps,
    it will be mended like that ramie thread.

     ANONYMOUS

Ramie thread is the fine fiber used in weaving the white or fawn "grass-cloth" of traditional Korean summer clothing.

228

Pass where the winds pause before going over,
   pass where the clouds pause before going over,
High peak of the pass of Changsŏng,
    where hand-reared falcons and
    wild-born falcons,
    peregrine falcons and yearling hawks,
    all pause before they cross.
If I knew that my love were over the pass,
    I should not pause a moment before I crossed.

     ANONYMOUS

Take your robe to pieces, make a coat and trousers,
        Take your rosary to pieces,
        make a donkey's crupper.
After ten years of studying
        the Realm of Sakyamuni, the Paradise of Bliss,
        the Boddhisattva Kwanseum,
        and "Nammu Amit'abul"
        now go your way.
In the night on a nun's breast
        you'll find no need to invoke the Buddha.

        ANONYMOUS

Sakyamuni is Gotama Buddha; the Paradise of Bliss is the heaven of
Mahayana Buddhism; Kwanseum is the Korean name of Avolokite-
shvara, the Boddhisattva of Mercy, usually known as Kwannon (Jap-
anese) or Kuan-yin (Chinese) or the "Goddess of Mercy" (though he
was originally a male, and in Korean temples often has moustaches);
"Nammu Amit'abul" is the Korean form of *Namah Amitabha*, the po-
tent invocation of the saving power of the Buddha of Light, which is
the commonest prayer of Korean Buddhism.

On that screen are painted a cat with its front teeth bared
        and a little mouse in front of the cat.
Oh, that cat looks a swift one.
        It is going to catch that mouse!
Shall I too see if I can find some bashful lover
        and try to catch him?

        ANONYMOUS

Spotted dog and black dog and shaggy blue hound—
>   but this yellow bitch is the wiliest in the pack.
Comes an unwanted guest
>   she'll wag her tail with pleasure
>   and follow behind his heels,
>   but for a friend of mine
>   she'll stiffen her legs and bare her teeth
>   and bark her head off.
>   You yellow bitch!
Tomorrow if I hear that man outside
>   shouting "Any dogs for sale?"
>   I'll tie you and sell you straight for dog meat.

ANONYMOUS

Of all the birds and all the beasts,
>   the cock and the dog are the ones to get rid of.
When my beloved is asleep at night
>   inside the green gauze screen,
>   the cock crows and makes him rise;
>   and when he comes stealthily outside my door,
>   the dog barks and makes him go away.
When the dog- or poultry-pedlar cries outside the gate,
>   I'll tie them up and sell them.

ANONYMOUS

The dog and the cock are traditionally esteemed by confucian poets for their ethical qualities, the regularity of the cock and the faithfulness of the dog. This fact adds to the satirical fun of the sasŏl sijo.

233

"Come and buy my dainties!"
            "Vendor, tell us what you're selling,
            then we'll see what we will buy!"
Bone outside and flesh inside it,
            both eyes looking up to heaven,
            going forwards, going backwards,
            eight feet on the little legs,
            two feet on the big ones,
            oh so tasty with green soy sauce,
            buy my splendid crab meat!"
"Vendor, do not cry such nonsense!
            Simply say, come buy my crabs."

ANONYMOUS

234

Mother-in-law, don't fume in the kitchen
            and swear at your daughter-in-law.
Did you get her in payment of a debt?
            Or did you buy her with cash?
            Father-in-law, tough as a rank shoot
            from a rotten chestnut stump,
            Mother-in-law, skinny and wrinkled
            as cowdung dried in the sun,
            Sister-in-law, sharp as a gimlet poking
            through the side of a three-year-old basket,
            your son has bloody faeces
            and is like weeds in a field of wheat,
            a miserable yellow cucumber flower.
How can you criticize a daughter-in-law
            who's like a morning glory
            blooming in loamy soil?

ANONYMOUS

How did it happen? However did it happen?

      Oh mother-in-law, what shall I do?

I was putting rice into the cauldron

      and the handle of the brass ladle broke!

      Oh mother-in-law, how did it happen?

There, now, girl; don't fuss so much,

      it often happened to me when I was young.

ANONYMOUS

A considerate mother-in-law was a contradiction of all traditional probability. The poem is therefore satirical.

236

Death-in-life girl, for heaven's sake
            stop frittering my innards!
Shall I give you money? Shall I give you silver?
                How many things shall I give you?
                A Chinese silk skirt, a Korean court dress,
                silk gauze petticoats and white satin belt,
                a gossamer twist of hair from the North.
                a jade hairpin, a bamboo hairpin,
                an amber-handled silver spatula,
                a golden spatula with a milky amber handle,
                a coral brooch from the southern seas,
                pure gold chopsticks engraved
                with heavenly peaches
                and hung with blue enamelled bells,
                a hairpin made of yellow pearls
                and embroidered shoes should I give you?
Silly one! That's a millionaire's dream:
                just give me one chance at that
                dimpling wrinkling cheek,
                lovely as a flower, but cheap at
                a thousand gold pieces!
                ANONYMOUS

237

A cauldron that cooks without fire,

A horse that grows fat without fodder,

> a concubine that weaves fine linen,
>
> a jug that fills itself with wine,
>
> a black cow that yields good tripe—
>
> o-o-u, o-o-u, u-hu-o-o!

If you can get these five things in life,

> you'll need to covet no more.

ANONYMOUS

The phrase here translated as "yields good tripe" has not been better explained. Its significance is far from clear. The whole poem is a good example of nonsense folk verse, but rounded off with a wry reflection on greed.

238

A green tree-frog died of a belly-ache,

> and on the night he died,

A gilded playboy of a toad offered the funeral requiem,

> a green grasshopper beat the side drum,
>
> a black locust played the ritual pipes,

And somewhere a crayfish carrying a pebble

> beat the rhythm of the big bass drum.

ANONYMOUS

Let's drink a cup of wine! And then drink another!
> Let's pluck flowers and lay them out
> to count off our endless cups!
Once your body is dead
> it will be bound in a straw mat
> and carried away on a jiggy,
> or sway in a brilliant bier followed
> by thousands of mourners,
> but still it will go to the reeds and the rushes,
> the oaks and the willows,
> where the sun shines yellow
> and the moon shines white,
> where fine rain falls
> and snowflakes whirl in the wind:
> and then who will say, "Let's drink a cup!"?
Some monkey will come and chatter on your grave,
> and what use will regrets be then?
> CHŎNG CH'ŎL (1536–1593)

A jiggy (Korean *chige*) is a wooden carrying-frame, held on the shoulders by straps of straw rope. It places the weight of the load in the center of a man's back, and is the ubiquitous equipment of farmers and laborers.

Naked children run along the stream
                waving hoops filled with cobwebs.
"Red dragonflies, red dragonflies!
                 If you go that way you'll die.
                 If you come this way you'll be all right!" they cry.
                 They themselves are dragonflies.
This is the way that all the world goes,
           I suppose.
                YI CHONGJIN (18th century)

"Idler, idler, indolent idler,
                lazy by day, lazy by night.
The golden cockerel painted on the wall
                flaps his wings, stretches his neck,
                and crows his heart out, lazybones!"
"Man is naught but morning dew.
                What else should we do but enjoy life?"
                ANONYMOUS

A white-headed playboy
                tried to act the handsome youth.
He dyed his hoary hair black
                and puffed his way up to a high mountain pass,
                but as he went over, a sudden shower
                made his white collar black
                and his black hair white.
And so the old fool's hopes
                were gained and lost again.
                ANONYMOUS

Three-month spring, do not boast of your colors,
  when flowers fade butterflies come no more.

Chao-chün's jade bones became the dirt of a Hun fortress,
The imperial concubine's fair face became the dust
    of the highway;
The blue pine and green bamboo endure for a thousand years,
But the green peach and the pink apricot
    last only a single spring.

Pretty maids may strive to keep their charms,
  but what use is the effort?

ANONYMOUS

The long middle section of this poem is in fact an independent poem written in Chinese, with purely Chinese grammar and Chinese allusions, according to the stylized T'ang conventions. It is composed of two couplets in each of which the structure of the two lines is exactly parallel. Chinese poetry of this sort was the poetry most frequently composed by Koreans during the period when sijo were also composed, and the quantity of Chinese poetry composed in Korea vastly exceeds the quantity of sijo.

Chao-chün was a beautiful concubine of the Han emperor who was sent as a bride to the Khan of the Huns in 33 B.C. Many legends have arisen about her name.

The imperial concubine, a reference no Korean would miss, is Yang Kuei-fei, the fabled concubine of the T'ang dynasty whose execution after the assassination of her emperor while they were fleeing has been the source of innumerable Chinese poems and stories.

The peony is the king of flowers
and the sunflower a noble subject;
The lotus is a gentleman,
the apricot blossom a commoner;
The chrysanthemum a sage in retirement,
the plum blossom a poor scholar;
The gourd flower is an old, old man,
the China pink is a boy;
The mallow is a witch
and the wild rose a harlot;
Among them the pear blossom is a poet,
and are not the red peach, the green peach,
and the peach of three colors,
all of them playboys?

ANONYMOUS

The three-colored peach is a flowering peach tree that has been known in Korean gardens for several centuries. The flowers are said to be red, pink, and white, all three colors on each branch, but in fact they are red, white, and red-and-white. The green peach is so-called because the fruit does not ripen for eating. Its multi-petaled flowers are white.

Modern Poems

In the slanting rays of the evening sun
>a boy on an ox plays his flute.
"If your ox bears no burden
>let it carry my worries."
"Taking them is easy enough:
>it's another thing to set them down."

HAN YONGUN (1879–1944)

Han Yongun was a distinguished buddhist monk and a leader of the Korean Independence Movement of 1919. This poem applies the ancient buddhist symbol of the soul portrayed as a boy on an ox to the poet's concern about his nation.

EPIGRAPH FOR A BROKEN INKSTONE

If it were broken in pieces,
            could it mend itself again?
Though it is no worse than cracked,
            and can still be used for grinding ink,
I wonder whether its sturdy heart
            is tingling from the pain?

CH'OE NAMSŎN (1886–1957)

Ch'oe Namsŏn was the reviver of sijo after the introduction of European literature into Korea in the twentieth century. He was also a distinguished koreanologist in other cultural and historical fields.

This poem is about an inkstone, used for grinding a Chinese inkstick in water immediately before writing or painting with a brush. It is one of the poems in *Paekp'al pŏnnoe*, which appeared in 1926 and was the first collection of modern sijo to be published. *Paekp'al pŏnnoe* means the one hundred and eight passions and delusions, the karmaic bonds of Buddhism.

247

Nothing but a bottle of medicine
            standing by the bedside table.
Not even a single visitor
            comes in with a bunch of flowers.
Being alone like this
            is sadder than being sick.

YI HOU (1912–1970)

Yi Hou, a journalist by profession, was a prolific writer of sijo who edited collections of classical poems. This is the second of three stanzas about a sickroom.

WAITING

Someone is beating on the door.

       ? ? ? ? ? ? ? ? ?

I hear it again.   ? ? ? ? ?

        I open it . . . .

Who's there. . . .? The door opens . . .

          Oh! It's only the rain. Rain. Only rain

      SIN SŬNGJU (1939–1964)

Sin Sŭngju liked to be called by his literary name Songp'a (Pine-Tree Slope.) He was the son of a herb doctor from Kangwon province and grew up in an east coast fishing village. As an undergraduate in Seoul he published a number of poems and won several prizes for poetry. He liked experimenting with the sijo form and produced such works as this one. He was not robust and died at the age of twenty-four of a liver disease while living very poorly in Seoul.

RETURN TO THE CAPITAL

Nine houses out of every ten

      have their doors nailed up.

But in the hearts of men

      there are more and bigger nails.

I find myself turning over in my mind

      all those nailed-up things.

      CH'OE NAMSŎN (1886–1957)

A poem written on returning to Seoul in February, 1951, after the expulsion of the communist army.

PANMUNJOM

So that's the brocaded landscape!

How come it's so cold and bare?

Nothing but rolled barbed wire

caught up in faded grasses.

Even say that wild flowers are music,

and that is a tale of the past.

Not very long ago here

there must have been a village too.

The rich tilth is going rotten,

no paddy, no dry fields,

A valley without sign of man:

only a few cranes strolling.

YI HANGNYŎNG (b. 1915)

Panmunjom is the site of the Korea Military Armistice Commission meetings.

251

You walked on the sand by the sea's edge

and left your footprints behind.

I keep tracing and retracing them,

even after the sun has gone down.

Tonight's tide will roll over them soon:

then they will all be washed away.

YI KWANGSU (b. 1892)

The author, a christian who became a buddhist, is regarded as the father of the modern Korean novel. He disappeared during the Korean war and is believed to have been taken to north Korea, and eventually to have died in a hospital in Peking in 1955.

Together with Ch'oe Namsŏn he pioneered the adoption of western modes of thought by Korean poets.

THE PUPPY

The puppy I got today
　　　　just sits in the room and howls.
I sat through the winter night
　　　　with my fingers incessantly sucked.
If this dog cannot be cured,
　　　　must I grow old sitting here?

YI HOU (1912–1970)

On this night the Magpie Bridge
　　　　will be built across the Milky Way,
The Herdboy and the Weaving Maid
　　　　will meet there just for once, they say.
All mankind aches desperately for
　　　　the Magpie Bridge and the Milky Way.

T'AK SANGSU (1900–1941)

The old Chinese legend tells how the Herdboy and the Weaving Maid, who spent too much time together, were banished as stars (Altair and Vega) to opposite banks of the Silver River (the Milky Way) but on the seventh night of the seventh moon every year the magpies form themselves into a bridge and allow the lovers to meet.

The poet never completed his schooling but published a number of sijo. He was drowned in a ferryboat accident off Chinhae.

254

Do not praise the Diamond Mountains,
        their glory is but crimson maples.
Red foliage can boast nothing
        but colors dying, leaf by leaf.
Go instead and look for happiness
        in the great winds of the Mongol Desert.

        SIN CH'AEHO (1880–1936)

Sin Ch'aeho was a distinguished patriot and historian who fled to Peking during the Japanese occupation, but finally died in prison. The Diamond Mountains are Korea's most celebrated natural beauty spot.

255

When dewdrops are pendant on
        the beards of the standing corn—
When the heads of broom beyond the wall
        are soaked and drooping in the rain—
At such times I cannot forget
        the days when we were together.

        YI KWANGSU (b. 1892)

256

The May moon casts close shadows

        through the fine mesh of the screen,

The white flowers of the blackthorn

        fill the air with heavy fragrance,

Everybody carries a candle,

        singing a hymn to Mary.

HA HANJU (b. 1909)

Ha Hanju is a Roman Catholic parish priest in a rural area who has used the sijo form to express the popular devotion of his church. He is one of the editors of *Sijo munhak* magazine. May is the month of Mary.

257

HIGH NOON

The song of the cicada ceases,

        the petals fall from the China rose.

In mid-heaven a solitary cloud

        seems to stop as it passes.

On the eaves that empty cobweb

        has not caught a single fly.

YI HOU (1912–1970)

The China rose (*Rosa chinensis*) is the traditional garden rose of Korea. It was used in the development of hybrid tea and floribunda types of rose.

MY HOME VILLAGE

When I quietly close my eyes, I see
    a twisting path across the meadows,
Where the water of the stream
    tumbles in runnels in the path,
And under the white poplars
    thatched houses hide behind brushwood fences.

I come leading a calf
    and see the azalea flowers
Covering the mountains all around
    like the pink evening glow of twilight;
And there is the heartening smell
    of the stew only mother can make.

The gentle girls will be gathering
    the savory mountain herbs
For the meal-table of every house
    in a village tasting the spring.
But when I open my eyes,
    my heart turns sad again.

KIM SANGOK (b. 1919)

Kim Sangok is one of the most successful modern writers of sijo. He is a schoolteacher and a novelist.

THE BUDDHIST MONK'S DANCE

Like a butterfly alighting,
   so that monk is coming down;
In wide cornette and long-sleeved robe,
   with stole flung round he dances down—
Butterfly with virgin tread
   very gently coming down.

Have flowers bloomed beneath the mountain
   that have not bloomed above?
He flies once, lands on a leaf;
   flies again, lights on a flower.
That monk is drunk with fragrance,
   he doesn't know where he is going.
   YANG SANGGYŎNG (b. 1904)

The poet is a herb doctor.

ORCHID

Full sprays of slender leaves
                    seem stiff, but are soft and supple;
The stocky purplish stalks
                    put out plain white flowers;
And the dew, turned into glass beads,
                    clings to every stem.

Inside, its true heart
                    delights in its purity;
It twists its roots deep down
                    between grains of clean white sand;
Far away from the slightest grime
                    it lives on the rain and the dew.

YI PYŎNGGI (1891–1968)

This poet was one of the most prolific modern writers of sijo and did much to encourage the art. Most of his work has the gentle touch of this piece, where the traditional moral approach to flowers is maintained in a modern idiom.

BLUE SKY

Sometimes feeling abstracted
                    I just gaze at the bright blue sky:
At the absolutely empty
                    blue sky, the wide blue sky.
And already it has entered my heart,
                    the wide blue bright blue sky.

YI ŬNSANG (b. 1903)

Yi Ŭnsang is well known by his pen name of Nosan (Egret Mountain) as a skillful writer of sijo poetry. His nature poems have a simple ease and directness as well as charming word music.

ON SIJO WRITING

The first line is a full skirt,
        the second is the bodice;
On reaching the third and last
        the neat collar has been added.
Lightly tie the ribbon bow,
        and the charm of the dress will appear.

The basic pattern of fours
        is like the counting of the days:
Twenty-eight will make a month,
        thirty-one, too, will make a month.
Set the stem, and when leaves and flowers bloom
        fragrance will come of itself.

The bright moon lighting up the sky,
        clear and white above the ground,
Is it just the shining soul
        of the sijo of ancient masters?
The mere sound of a lute in moonlight
        is that not a sijo too?

        YANG SANGGYŎNG (b. 1904)

The first stanza is a careful description of a Korean woman's dress, which consists of a very full skirt and a bodice tied over the right breast with a broad long bow or ribbon. The basic pattern of fours refers to the number of syllables in each phrase.

THE MOUNTAIN STREAM

The clear stream trickles
           in the pinewoods' shade,
The high branches
           catch the slanting sunlight,
The fine leaves shimmer
           like dazzling silver needles.

Two or three turquoise tiles
           are set in the temple roof,
No birds come flying
           in the courtyards, back or front,
The water trickles in the gulley,
           burbling to itself.

The sand gets rinsed again and again,
           till every grain is polished,
The rocks are worn and worn away,
           engraved like precious stones,
And yet, as though they should be soiled again,
           the stream forever washes them.

Hear the sound of the waterfall!
           Stop your ears and look!
Make a pillow of a stone,
           and lying on the sand
Shade the sun with one hand
           and look at the blue vault of heaven.

Rocks piled on rocks,
           embracing rocks, bearing rocks,
And the valley twisting,
           now narrow, now wide,
Cares and tiredness fall away
           as I walk up the plashing stream.

But steep, how steep
           is the path we climb.
The sound of the water has ceased
           and the white clouds have appeared:
The peak we looked up to from below
           is now beneath our feet.
           YI PYŎNGGI (1891–1968)

264

I WILL WRITE A POEM TOO

Up above the shimmering sea
           two or three seagulls are hovering.
Rolling, wheeling, they write a poem.
           I do not know the alphabet they use.
On the broad expanse of sky
           I will write a poem too.
           YI ŬNSANG (b. 1903)

Reference Material

TEXTS AND SOURCES

The written texts of classic sijo have come down to us in two groups: those contained in the posthumous collected works of particular authors, and those edited in the anthologies made for singers. The two groups provide quite different problems for the literary historian.

The poems which are contained in the posthumous editions of individual authors (for it was rare for a man's works to be printed in his lifetime) have the surest claims to authenticity. Thus the sijo of Chŏng Ch'ŏl (d. 1593) are nearly all included in *Songgang kasa* ("The Lyrics of Songgang"), which was published five times between 1690 and 1768. Those of Yun Sŏndo (d. 1671) are to be found in *Kosan chip* ("The Collected Works of Kosan"), first published in 1791, and some other manuscripts. These can, despite the variant readings of the editions, confidently be accepted as the work of the poets to whom they are attributed. The same is true of the poems of Pak Inno (d. 1642), although his collected works, *Nogye chip*, were not published until 1800.

These are the three major poets in the sijo genre during the Yi dynasty. The quantity of their output and the quality of their work—in spite of some reservations about the didacticism of Nogye—make them the finest representatives of the great period of the fifteenth to seventeenth centuries.

There are other men whose sijo have been handed down in the same fashion, but none of them is represented in this collection of translations.

The *Tosan sibi ka* ("The Twelve Songs of Tosan") by Yi Hwang (T'oegye) are a special case. They are recorded on four wooden printing blocks still preserved at his home and shrine at Tosan Sŏwŏn, near Andong in North Kyŏngsang province. Impressions are taken of the blocks for visitors while they wait. The four blocks are believed to have been carved from T'oegye's own handwriting in 1565. They are thus the oldest existing written version of any sijo.

These men were all known from other writings, and the internal evidence of the sijo is consistent with the traditional attributions of authorship. In the case of Yi I (otherwise called Yulgok; d. 1584), whose *Kosan ku kokka* ("The Nine Songs of Kosan") are fully in accord with the rest of his thinking, the earliest text we have of the songs is from an anthology compiled two hundred and fifty years after his death. In spite of some corroborative evidence in the form of Chinese verse translations of the songs by other people, there must always be some doubt as to how far the texts we now have represent what Yulgok wrote.

The second group of texts comprises the anthologies, which began to be compiled in the eighteenth century. They were made for singers, and were copied by hand. Their value varies considerably, and they represent a partial crystallizing of the oral tradition. There are many variations in the text of the same song as it appears in different anthologies, and a large number of songs are so nearly the same as others as to cast doubt on their right to exist as independent compositions. Both these facts indicate that the tradition was not a meticulous one. In some cases it is clear that the singers did not know the real meaning of the earlier versions of a poem and so changed it when they came to write it down.

The three greatest anthologies are the *Ch'ŏnggu yŏngŏn* ("Long-drawn-out Words of the Green Hills". Long-drawn-out—i.e., chanted—words is a quotation from the *Shu ching*, the Chinese *Book of Documents*, and means songs; Green Hills is an ancient Chinese name for a fairyland in the eastern sea which has become a sobriquet for Korea. The name therefore means simply "Korean Songs.") of 1728; the *Haedong kayo* ("Songs from Beyond the Eastern Sea," i.e., "of Korea") of 1769; and the *Kagok wŏllyu* ("Source and Flow of Songs"), finished in 1876.

Ch'ŏnggu yŏngŏn was the first and set the standard for all subsequent sijo anthologies. It was edited by Kim Ch'ŏnt'aek, a professional singer. The text now known as the *chinbon*, or "original text," contains 580 songs, arranged according to the tunes to which they were sung, though the arrangement within some of the melodic groupings is by subject matter. The names of the authors are given where they were known to the compiler. Chinese characters are mixed with Korean letters in the script.

Several other collections called *Ch'ŏnggu yŏng'ŏn*, having more or less similarity to the original anthology of the name, exist and have been reprinted in this century. The largest contains 998 songs, some of them of obviously legendary origin. Yet another book, dating from 1815, has only 257 pieces, again with some highly improbable imputations of authorship, and the whole without any proper order. A third *Ch'ŏnggu yŏngŏn*, with 727 songs, proves to be a version of the nineteenth-century anthology *Kagok wŏllyu*. In fact *Ch'ŏnggu yŏngŏn* came to be a title applied indiscriminately to sijo anthologies.

The *Haedong kayo* was edited by Kim Sujang, with the poems arranged by author. The work seems to have been done in three stages between 1746 and 1769. Two different versions exist: the earlier one has 568 songs and the later one 638.

Both the *Ch'ŏnggu yŏngŏn* and the *Haedong kayo* contain much material which they attribute to contemporaries of the anthologists. There is little reason to doubt that such works are properly attributed. These two anthologies do not claim any authorship earlier than the latter end of the Koryŏ dynasty. Later anthologies often attributed poems, quite incredibly, to much earlier periods. The sober time range of the *Ch'ŏnggu yŏngŏn* and the *Haedong kayo* argues in favor of the general soundness of their traditional attributions, which have been accepted by the majority of Korean scholars until very recently, though it is recognized now that there is some room for doubt.

The *Kagok wŏllyu* of 1876 was intended to be a definitive collection of the best songs, arranged according to the melodies. It includes works by nineteenth-century authors, especially the editors, Pak Hyogwan and An Minyŏng. Some copies of it have different titles, such as *Kasa chip* ("Collection of Songs"), *Haedong akchang*, and *Ch'ŏnggu akchang* ("Songs of. the Green Hills"), but these may have been applied to copies which have lost their original covers. On the other hand, the name *Kagok wŏllyu* is really the heading to a passage about the history of songs in China, which is set as a preface to the book. It is quoted

159

from the *Neng-kai-chai man-lu*, a collection of essays by the Chinese Sung dynasty writer Wu Ts'eng. There are several versions of the *Kagok wŏllyu*. The best have 660 songs, with an appendix of 180 or 190 songs for woman's voice (*yŏch'ang yuch'wi* or *yŏch'ang chil*). Many scholars regarded this as the best organized of the three great anthologies.

The other anthologies that were made before the introduction of western printing methods into Korea date from the nineteenth century. They are generally inferior to the three collections just discussed, and in great part repeat the same material. Their interest lies in the variant readings they produce, their witness to the nature of the oral tradition, and the poems in them which are not to be found elsewhere. The use of sobriquets for "Korea," like *Ch'ŏnggu* and *Haedong*, in many of their titles was probably intended to indicate that the songs are of a peculiarly Korean type and written in the Korean language, rather than in Chinese.

The *Kogŭm kagok* ("Songs Ancient and Modern"), which may date from as early as 1764, but more probably from 1824, has 302 sijo, arranged according to subject matter by the otherwise unknown Songgye-yŏnwŏl. More than one-third of them are missing from the great anthologies. (The original of this anthology is in the library of the University of California at Berkeley.)

The *Kŭnhwa akpu* ("Hibiscus Flower Music Book"— "hibiscus flower" also refers to Korea) of 1779 or 1839 has 394 poems arranged according to subject matter. The *Pyŏngwa kagok chip* ("Pyŏngwa's Song Collection") was discovered in 1956 in a village near Yŏngch'ŏn in North Kyŏngsang province. It is named after Pyŏngwa (Yi Hyŏngsang, 1653–1733), among whose reliques it was preserved, though it almost certainly belongs to a later period. It is a vast collection of 1,109 poems, 78 of which are not found in other anthologies.

Namhun t'aep'yŏng-ga ("Songs of Prosperity on the Southern Breeze"—the name refers to ancient poems about the auspicious southern breezes of the golden age of the Emperor Shun) is a text for singers—printed by woodblocks—written in 1803 or 1863. It contains 224 sijo, arranged according to melody and even spelled out for singing rather than according to the normal orthography.

Authors are not named and the last foot of each poem, which is never sung, is omitted. This was the book from which James S. Gale made the first translations of sijo published in English. *Siga yogok* ("Lyric Songs") is another singing text, from the last quarter of the nineteenth century. *Yŏch'ang kayo rok* ("Texts of Songs for Woman's Voice"), dated 1870 or later, is a textbook for pupils learning to sing. It has only 143 songs. *Tongga sŏn* ("Selection of Eastern [i.e., Korean] Songs"), undated, has 235 poems arranged according to their melodies, with a note after each one classifying it according to subject matter.

Hwawŏn akpo ("Music of the Flower Springs"—a title probably referring to the Peach Blossom Spring mentioned in translation No. 190 of this book), probably written in 1907, has 650 songs, many with spurious early attributions. The *Taedong p'unga* ("Music of the Great Orient" [i.e., of Korea]) with 321 poems was printed by Kim Kyohŏn in 1908.

From this point on, the printed sijo anthologies begin to proliferate. They vary from small collections of the most famous songs to comprehensive collections attempting to canonize the whole sijo literature. The primary concern is no longer with the sijo as songs, but with sijo as literature.

The pioneer comprehensive collection was Ch'oe Namsŏn's *Sijo yuch'wi* ("Sijo Anthology") of 1928. It contains 1,405 poems arranged according to subject matter. Another comprehensive publication is the *Kyoju kagok chip* ("Annotated Collection of Songs"), edited by the Japanese scholar Maema Kyosaku, in which the contents of ten of the earlier anthologies are collated. It contains 1,789 poems, arranged under authors' names in chronological order, except for the anonymous songs, which are classified by melody. It was published in 1951. A very large collection, though the scanty notes are of poor quality, is the *Han'guk sijo chip* by Han Yongsŏn in 1963. It contains 2,015 poems classified according to subject matter. Many of the poems are doublets.

The best modern collection is the *Sijo munhak sajŏn* ("Dictionary of Sijo Literature"), edited by Chŏng Pyŏnguk, which was published in 1966. It contains 2,376 poems, arranged in alphabetical order of the opening words. It gives a full account of the source of each poem in published books, though it does not give textual variants. It has succinct but very useful notes on authors, anthologies, the meanings of obscure words and Chinese phrases, and copious indexes. It is indispensable for serious students, and I have made constant use of it in preparing this work.

There are several cyclostyled editions of the pre-twentieth century anthologies, and there is now a vast literature of annotated selections of sijo designed for use by students. The magazine *Sijo munhak*, which has been published irregularly since June, 1960, is chiefly concerned with modern sijo writing, but sometimes has articles on the older compositions, which are studied more regularly in the journals of the Korean language and literature specialists.

Modern sijo also appear in *Ch'ŏngja* ("Celadon"), published occasionally since 1965 by a group of poets centered on Taejon. The Sijo Writers' Club (Han'guk sijo chakcha hyŏphoe) produces annual anthologies. Its recent anthology *Hansan sŏm*, in honor of Yi Sunsin, contains a poem by the President of the Republic.

This account of the history of sijo publication will have made it clear that apart from the dozen or so authors whose poems were printed before the anthologists began their work in the eighteenth century, the attribution of earlier sijo rests solely on tradition and has no literary evidence to support it. Nor can we determine the original texts with certainty, since we have only eighteenth-century versions of poems said to have been written as much as four centuries earlier.

One example is of particular interest. The famous sijo by Yi Sunsin (No. 9 in this volume) is not found in his "Complete Works" (*Yi Ch'ungmu-gong chŏnsŏ*), published in 1795, and widely differing versions of it exist. There is a Chinese poem with the same meaning in the *chŏnsŏ*; and two entries in his war diary, *Nanjung ilgi*, describe similar events. It is impossible to say for certain whether the Chinese poem is a translation from the sijo, or whether the sijo was composed by a professional singer on the basis of the Chinese poem. Korean sentiment naturally tends to the belief that the great admiral composed the Korean-language poem himself. Our earliest text of the sijo dates from 1728, when it was included in the *Ch'ŏnggu yŏngŏn*. It is therefore surprising that it found no place in the admiral's complete works published in 1795. The literary investigator has room for doubt about the true origin of the poem.

The translator who is concerned with literary pleasure rather than with literary history can afford to be eclectic, and the texts used for the translations in this book were chosen for aesthetic, not historical, reasons. The variant readings have not yet been properly studied, and no objective criterion has been established which could be applied in compiling a book like this.

To enable readers of Korean to trace the texts of the older poems I have indicated in two indexes their numbers in Chŏng Pyŏnguk's *Sijo munhak sajŏn* (mentioned above, and published in Seoul by Sin'gu munhwa-sa in 1966). The two poems not so referenced are not in that book; but No. 67 is in Ch'oe Namsŏn's *Sijo yuch'wi* (No. 445). I have not discovered No. 90 in any published anthology.

There is no authoritative collection containing all the modern pieces. I have provided references so far as possible to *Hyŏndae sijo sŏnch'ong* ("Selection of Modern Sijo"), edited by Yi Pyŏnggi and Yi T'aegŭk (Seoul: Saegŭl-sa, 1958). This is still the most useful anthology of twentieth-century sijo. The sijo contained in it were originally published elsewhere, often in the collected works of authors.

Old sijo rarely have titles, apart from the titles of the cycles. Modern writers sometimes give their sijo titles and sometimes they do not. I have tried to follow the practice of the author so far as I could discover it.

In the following tables the corresponding numbers of the Korean texts in Chŏng Pyŏnguk's *Sijo munhak sajŏn* and the translations in this book are set out in two orders: first in the numerical order of the translations for help in identifying the original; and then in the numerical order of the texts in Professor Chŏng's dictionary to help in discovering whether a text has been included in this volume.

Rutt Chŏng			
1. 890	42. 423	85. 1396	128. 2055
2. 2371	43. 222	86. 1423	129. 733
3. 1036	44. 157	87. 965	130. 226
4. 2110	45. 646	88. 1411	131. 1605
5. 2128	46. 332	89. 334	132. 2075
6. 1987	47. 1816	91. 45	133. 811
7. 1951	48. 1383	92. 1574	134. 976
8. 61	49. 2301	93. 1023	135. 807
9. 2267	50. 992	94. 1955	136. 356
10. 2149	51. 520	95. 304	137. 2247
11. 2053	52. 660	96. 353	138. 1921
12. 2038	53. 836	97. 52	139. 142
13. 1858	54. 1847	98. 1496	140. 1729
14. 2232	55. 1236	99. 913	141. 1633
15. 1413	56. 1666	100. 1273	142. 1070
16. 93	57. 1665	101. 317	143. 993
17. 1392	58. 816	102. 114	144. 1484
18. 2157	59. 2226	103. 113	145. 1624
19. 2231	60. 236	104. 148	146. 2173
20. 833	61. 419	105. 402	147. 2207
21. 1328	62. 751	106. 2087	148. 216
22. 599	63. 1221	107. 654	149. 2044
23. 1821	64. 2366	108. 661	150. 1873
24. 166	65. 979	109. 1050	151. 1489
25. 115	66. 2063	110. 831	152. 2066
26. 1418	68. 735	111. 1404	153. 2310
27. 1540	69. 1594	112. 712	154. 1309
28. 716	70. 1427	113. 98	155. 770
29. 1697	71. 853	114. 620	156. 677
30. 1133	72. 255	115. 536	157. 488
31. 15	73. 1013	116. 1719	158. 1485
32. 247	74. 254	117. 1359	159. 1106
33. 2195	75. 1575	118. 1952	160. 1536
34. 946	76. 774	119. 1760	161. 1941
35. 122	77. 672	120. 62	162. 1942
36. 1725	78. 597	121. 210	163. 742
37. 1911	79. 738	122. 762	164. 636
38. 1527	80. 1444	123. 2374	165. 1061
39. 1272	81. 377	124. 202	166. 1062
40. 2294	82. 286	125. 888	167. 1329
41. 855	83. 1263	126. 1700	168. 1331
	84. 1180	127. 737	169. 1333

170.	1332	189.	866	208.	469	227.	768
171.	1640	190.	2169	209.	2375	228.	825
172.	1477	191.	348	210.	119	229.	1793
173.	1237	192.	439	211.	1541	230.	920
174.	1616	193.	233	212.	1218	231.	821
175.	1053	194.	1469	213.	221	232.	980
176.	2159	195.	709	214.	1887	233.	643
177.	1999	196.	814	215.	1464	234.	1271
178.	503	197.	724	216.	59	235.	1409
179.	145	198.	316	217.	277	236.	1109
180.	612	199.	1135	218.	1766	237.	972
181.	2065	200.	771	219.	583	238.	2040
182.	1578	201.	860	220.	813	239.	2281
183.	1352	202.	1544	221.	1969	240.	857
184.	369	203.	799	222.	1398	241.	475
185.	679	204.	1226	223.	667	242.	880
186.	1571	205.	894	224.	330	243.	1081
187.	144	206.	299	225.	909	244.	766
188.	1136	207.	1626	226.	1856		

Chồng	Rutt						
15.	31	356.	136	770.	155	1070.	142
45.	91	369.	184	771.	200	1081.	243
52.	97	377.	81	774.	76	1106.	159
59.	216	402.	105	799.	203	1109.	236
61.	8	419.	61	807.	135	1133.	30
62.	120	423.	42	811.	133	1135.	199
93.	16	439.	192	813.	220	1136.	188
98.	113	469.	208	814.	196	1180.	84
113.	103	475.	241	816.	58	1218.	212
114.	102	488.	157	821.	231	1221.	63
115.	25	503.	178	825.	228	1226.	204
119.	210	520.	51	831.	110	1236.	55
122.	35	536.	115	833.	20	1237.	173
142.	139	583.	219	836.	53	1263.	83
144.	187	597.	78	853.	71	1271.	234
145.	179	599.	22	855.	41	1272.	39
148.	104	612.	180	857.	240	1273.	100
157.	44	620.	114	860.	201	1309.	154
166.	24	636.	164	866.	189	1328.	21
202.	124	643.	233	880.	242	1329.	167
210.	121	646.	45	888.	125	1331.	168
216.	148	654.	107	890.	1	1332.	170
221.	213	660.	52	894.	205	1333.	169
222.	43	661.	108	909.	225	1352.	183
226.	130	667.	223	913.	99	1359.	117
233.	193	672.	77	920.	230	1383.	48
236.	60	677.	156	946.	34	1392.	17
247.	32	679.	185	965.	87	1396.	85
254.	74	709.	195	972.	237	1398.	222
255.	72	712.	112	976.	134	1404.	111
277.	217	716.	28	979.	65	1409.	235
286.	82	724.	197	980.	232	1411.	88
299.	206	733.	129	992.	50	1413.	15
304.	95	735.	68	993.	143	1418.	26
316.	198	737.	127	1013.	73	1423.	86
317.	101	738.	79	1023.	93	1427.	70
330.	224	742.	163	1036.	3	1444.	80
332.	46	751.	62	1050.	109	1464.	215
334.	89	762.	122	1053.	175	1469.	194
348.	191	766.	244	1061.	165	1477.	172
353.	96	768.	227	1062.	166	1484.	144

1485.	158	1666.	56	1951.	7	2157.	18
1489.	151	1697.	29	1952.	118	2159.	176
1496.	98	1700.	126	1955.	94	2169.	190
1527.	38	1719.	116	1969.	221	2173.	146
1536.	160	1725.	36	1987.	6	2195.	33
1540.	27	1729.	140	1999.	177	2207.	147
1541.	211	1760.	119	2038.	12	2226.	59
1544.	202	1766.	218	2040.	238	2231.	19
1571.	186	1793.	229	2044.	149	2232.	14
1574.	92	1816.	47	2053.	11	2247.	137
1575.	75	1821.	23	2055.	128	2267.	9
1578.	182	1847.	54	2063.	66	2281.	239
1594.	69	1856.	226	2065.	181	2294.	40
1605.	131	1858.	13	2066.	152	2301.	49
1616.	174	1873.	150	2075.	132	2310.	153
1624.	145	1887.	214	2087.	106	2366.	64
1626.	207	1911.	37	2110.	4	2371.	2
1633.	141	1921.	138	2128.	5	2374.	123
1640.	171	1941.	161	2149.	10	2375.	209
1665.	57	1942.	162				

245 HHS p. 286
246 HHS p. 257. Originally in Paekp'al pŏnnoe, 1926.
247 Yi Hou sijo chip, 1955, p. 96
248 Sijo munhak, XI, 48. (Posthumously printed May, 1965.)
249 HSS p. 257
250 Sijo munhak, VII, 48 (March, 1963)
251 HSS p. 144. From Ch'unwŏn siga chip (posthumously printed, 1955).
252 Yi Hou sijo chip, 1955, p. 112
253 HSS p. 278. Originally in Tonga ilbo, August 10, 1927.
254 Kŏgŭm myŏng sijo chŏnghae, 1954, p. 395

255 HSS p. 146. From Ch'unwŏn siga chip (posthumously printed, 1955).
256 Madonna, 1960, p. 138
257 HSS p. 197. Yi Hou sijo chip, p. 83.
258 HSS p. 13. Originally in Ch'ojŏk, 1947.
259 HSS p. 134. Originally in Ch'ulpŏm, 1947.
260 HSS p. 155. Originally in Karam sijo chip, 1938.
261 Nosan sijo sŏnjip, 1958, p. 377. (Written 1940.)
262 HSS p. 134. Originally in Ch'ulpŏm, 1947.
263 HSS p. 152
264 Nosan sijo sŏnjip, 1958, p. 374. (Written 1938.)

INDEX OF AUTHORS

INDEX OF FIRST LINES

Ann Arbor Paperbacks

Waddell, *The Desert Fathers*
Erasmus, *The Praise of Folly*
Donne, *Devotions*
Malthus, *Population: The First Essay*
Berdyaev, *The Origin of Russian Communism*
Einhard, *The Life of Charlemagne*
Edwards, *The Nature of True Virtue*
Gilson, *Héloïse and Abélard*
Aristotle, *Metaphysics*
Kant, *Education*
Boulding, *The Image*
Duckett, *The Gateway to the Middle Ages*
    (3 vols.): *Italy; France and Britain;
    Monasticism*
Bowditch and Ramsland, *Voices of the
    Industrial Revolution*
Luxemburg, *The Russian Revolution* and
    Leninism or Marxism?
Rexroth, *Poems from the Greek Anthology*
Zoshchenko, *Scenes from the Bathhouse*
Thrupp, *The Merchant Class of Medieval
    London*
Procopius, *Secret History*
Adcock, *Roman Political Ideas and Practice*
Swanson, *The Birth of the Gods*
Xenophon, *The March Up Country*
Trotsky, *The New Course*
Buchanan and Tullock, *The Calculus of
    Consent*
Hobson, *Imperialism*
Pobedonostsev, *Reflections of a Russian
    Statesman*
Kinietz, *The Indians of the Western Great
    Lakes 1615–1760*
Bromage, *Writing for Business*
Lurie, *Mountain Wolf Woman, Sister of
    Crashing Thunder*
Leonard, *Baroque Times in Old Mexico*
Meier, *Negro Thought in America,
    1880–1915*
Burke, *The Philosophy of Edmund Burke*
Michelet, *Joan of Arc*
Conze, *Buddhist Thought in India*
Arberry, *Aspects of Islamic
    Civilization*
Chesnutt, *The Wife of His Youth and
    Other Stories*
Gross, *Sound and Form in Modern Poetry*
Zola, *The Masterpiece*
Chesnutt, *The Marrow of Tradition*
Aristophanes, *Four Comedies*
Aristophanes, *Three Comedies*
Chesnutt, *The Conjure Woman*
Duckett, *Carolingian Portraits*

Rapoport and Chammah, *Prisoner's Dilemma*
Aristotle, *Poetics*
Peattie, *The View from the Barrio*
Duckett, *Death and Life in the Tenth Century*
Langford, *Galileo, Science and the Church*
McNaughton, *The Taoist Vision*
Anderson, *Matthew Arnold and the Classical
    Tradition*
Milio, *9226 Kercheval*
Weisheipl, *The Development of Physical
    Theory in the Middle Ages*
Breton, *Manifestoes of Surrealism*
Gershman, *The Surrealist Revolution in
    France*
Burt, *Mammals of the Great Lakes Region*
Lester, *Theravada Buddhism in Southeast Asia*
Scholz, *Carolingian Chronicles*
Wik, *Henry Ford and Grass-roots America*
Sahlins and Service, *Evolution and Culture*
Wickham, *Early Medieval Italy*
Waddell, *The Wandering Scholars*
Rosenberg, *Bolshevik Visions* (2 parts in 2
    vols.)
Mannoni, *Prospero and Caliban*
Aron, *Democracy and Totalitarianism*
Shy, *A People Numerous and Armed*
Taylor, *Roman Voting Assemblies*
Goodfield, *An Imagined World*
Hesiod, *The Works and Days; Theogony; The
    Shield of Herakles*
Raverat, *Period Piece*
Lamming, *In the Castle of My Skin*
Fisher, *The Conjure-Man Dies*
Strayer, *The Albigensian Crusades*
Lamming, *The Pleasures of Exile*
Lamming, *Natives of My Person*
Glaspell, *Lifted Masks and Other Works*
Wolff, *Aesthetics and the Sociology of Art*
Grand, *The Heavenly Twins*
Cornford, *The Origin of Attic Comedy*
Allen, *Wolves of Minong*
Brathwaite, *Roots*
Fisher, *The Walls of Jericho*
Lamming, *The Emigrants*
Loudon, *The Mummy!*
Kemble and Butler Leigh, *Principles and
    Privilege*
Thomas, *Out of Time*
Flanagan, *You Alone Are Dancing*
Kotre and Hall, *Seasons of Life*
Shen, *Almost a Revolution*
Meckel, *Save the Babies*
Laver and Schofield, *Multiparty Government*
Rutt, *The Bamboo Grove*